Tom Bentley

Think Like a Writer

How to Write the Stories You See

First published by The Write Word in 2015.

First Edition.

ISBN: 978-1-927967-79-9

This book was professionally typeset on Reedsy.
Find out more at reedsy.com

Contents

1

Introduction

> *Think of your favorite book. No, better yet, go and get your favorite book, feel its heft in your hand, flip through its pages, smell its bookness. Read a passage or two to send that stream of sparks through your head, the alchemy that occurs when the written word collides with the chemicals of your consciousness: Delight is the fruit of that collision.*

When I was seven or eight years old, I'd walk to the nearby public library, and go into the section on dinosaurs. I would lie in the aisle for hours, surrounded by scattered stacks of books, driving through a landscape of imagination, fueled by words. At first, I was simply thrilled by the stories of the great beasts, but after a time, I began to realize that I was taken by the words themselves—Jurassic, Triceratops, Tyrannosaurus—and would say them softly aloud.

Many, many books later, it began to dawn on me that books were the conscious, choice-making work of authors. I started to fathom that a writer employed tools, framed a composition, shaped its architecture.

Deeper yet, that writing had a voice, that it was animated by a current.

When I was twelve years old, I was swimming in the ocean and was tugged out by a small rip current that took me, amidst slamming waves, against the supports of a public pier. I screamed for help at the people looking down at me; no one seemed to react. I was terrified that I would die, while enraged that no one cared. In my agitation, I didn't know that someone had called a lifeguard, who quickly rescued me.

A Pin That Poked Deeply

Months later, for a class assignment, I wrote an essay in which I described in detail my fear, fury and despair. My teacher later read the story aloud, saying it was a vivid slice of life. At the end of the year, the school handed out student awards, and I was given a little cloisonné pin that said "Best Writer." I knew before then that writing had an unusual power over me, but the commendation told me that language, even my language, could hold sway over others as well.

I read broadly, though wrote only sporadically.

When I was fifteen, my parents granted me the indulgence of letting a friend paint, in a nice cursive script, the final page of Hesse's Siddhartha on the wall, floor to ceiling, facing my bed. I thought that constantly reading those mindful words would prompt some spiritual renaissance. My other teenage absorptions checked that vow, but my interest in the power of words increased all the more.

Hesse said in an essay: " ... I want to dream myself into priests and wanderers, female cooks and murderers, children and animals, and, more than anything else, birds and trees ... " To me, he's talking about the force of imagination, the authority of an authentic voice.

More and more, I came to see that the world of imagination is the biggest world there is, and that a writer can write to see the unexpected, to know the hidden, to do as Asimov suggested and "think through his fingers." And that words can be so sensual you want to lick them.

Once Upon A Time ...

I saw evidence everywhere that people were storytellers. They have been storytellers for ages, whether the words were inscribed on resistant stone, delivered in a lilting voice or caught in an electronic dance. I knew I wanted to be a storyteller too. However, I was still striking the anvil of ideas with brute blows, yet to learn the deft stitchings and tight knots in narrative's fabric. But I wasn't discouraged enough not to write. I tried poems, short stories, personal essays and more.

Twenty-five years ago, the *San Francisco Chronicle* accepted my article on my then 15-year correspondence with the Jack Daniel's Distillery, publishing it in the beloved "Sunday Punch" section. I bought 10 copies, and sat on a bench in Golden Gate Park just staring at my byline, not even reading the article. Still not literature, not the stuff of Lear's stormy fulminations, of Conrad's lurid Congo, of Twain's beckoning twang, but for me, word magic.

I finally realized that I couldn't wait for inspiration, a muse whose answering machine is all I got when I called. So, since then, a couple of novels, a small-press published collection of short stories, a big basketful of essays and articles, a new novel in s-l-o-w progress—but nearly written. And this book.

I write because language is a bright bird, uncatchable, but worth every attempt.

Confessions of a Word Drunk

I want to share that sense of being word-drunk with you, how to open the bottle and pour yourself a glass. This book is about how to recognize—nay, *invoke* your writing voice, how to see stories everywhere, how to net those elusive butterflies and imprint them on the page. I'll start the show by sliding the big platter of "how to find your writing voice" and "how to see with a writer's eyes" into the center of the table.

Then, there will be a palate cleanser on my own writing background as it relates to the writing life. Then, piping hot, a savory side dish about what works in the writing life: how to coax (or more accurately, throttle back and direct) your writing ideas, and how to sidestep writing distractions. Then let's share some dessert sugared with how to work with different writing structures (from their very letters to words to paragraphs, oh my! Characters and stories too).

Best to conclude with post-prandial cognac: the practical matters of writing tools and other writing resources, including links online to bright writing minds.

Let's head to that savory writing table.

PS Oh, before I open my mouth in print, let it be proclaimed that I'm a bit of a wise guy. Duck if you see a bad joke flying at you.

2

Don't Muzzle (or Muffle) Your Writing Voice

> *I think about the issue of voice in writing quite often. You know, your writing voice, that whiff of brimstone or reverberant cello note or cracked teeth and swollen tongue that stamps your writing as having been issued from you alone. Many writers, particularly younger ones, struggle to find their voice: the word choice, the cadence, the tone, the very punctuation—the stuff that slyly suggests or that screams that you wrote it.*

You'd never mistake Donald Barthelme for Ernest Hemingway; the word blossoms gathered in Virginia Woolf's garden would have flowers not found in the window-box plantings of Joan Didion. So your writing and your writing voice shouldn't be confused with Schlomo Bierbaum's—it should be yours alone.

One of the things that made me think of a person's voice was a literal voice: a few years ago I saw Ricki Lee Jones in concert, and was so struck by her uniqueness as a performer (and possibly as a person). She was cuckoo and mesmerizing in the best of ways on stage: banging on the roof of the piano, exhorting the other players, talking to them in asides during some songs. She played a lunatic version of *Don't Fear the Reaper(!)*, beating out a slapclap on the top of her piano. The performance was so Rikki Lee Jones: singular, eccentric, passionate, moody. You wanted to be around her just to see what she might do or say (or sing) next. Her voice was hers and hers alone.

Your Writing Voice Is There for the Singing

When you're developing your writing voice, you might be so painstakingly wrapped up in expressing yourself JUST SO that you drain the blood out of your writing, or pull the plug on the electricity of your ideas. You might have read an essay by Pico Iyer or a story by Alice Munro or a novel by Cormac McCarthy and you might be trying so hard to source and employ the rhythms, humors and tics of those gifted writers that you spill onto the page a fridge full of half-opened condiments that cancel each other's flavors.

Be yourself behind the pen, be the channel between what cooks in your brain and what courses through the keyboard. Even if that self is one day the grinning jester and another the sentimental fool, be fully that person, unmasked, on the page. Maybe you grew up in a slum in Mumbai or have a pied-à-terre in every European capital, maybe your adolescence was a thing of constant pain, maybe you never made a wrong move, maybe you never moved at all—it should be in your writing, whether in its proclamations or its subtext. Your voice is all the Crayons in your box.

For instance, if you're inclined to the confessional (like all us old Catholics), turn to your sins: I was a very enterprising shoplifter in high school, running a cottage resale business on the side. While I don't recommend they teach my techniques in business school, I later forged my history of happy hands into an award-winning short story, and then turned the account of having won that short story contest[1] into a published article in a Writer's Market volume. Ahh, the just desserts of an empire of crime.

A Voice, and Its Chorus

Of course it's no monotone: Sometimes I might write about Sisyphus and sometimes I might write about drool (and sometimes I might speculate whether Sisyphus drooled while pushing the rock up that endless hill). By that I mean your short stories might have a female narrators, male narrators, be set in a tiny town one time and in a howling metropolis the next. But you still must find the voice—*your* voice—for that story.

I like to write essays that often take a humorous slant, but at the same time, that isn't the limit or restriction I put on my own expression. I published a piece on not actually knowing my father despite my years with him, and another that discusses[2] never finding out what happened to my high school girlfriend after she vanished in Colombia. Both had a tone of pathos. That pensive tone is also one of my voices, and its sobriety doesn't cancel the chiming of my comic voice. So your voice might be part of a choir.

---

1 http://www.tombentley.com/CrimePays.pdf

2 http://www.ourpastloves.com/2014-contest-winners

Getting Gritty About Grammar

A friend of mine who was putting together a "private university" once asked me if I would teach a 16-session class on grammar, because of what she perceived as the lamentable state of comprehension of language structures and their underpinnings among the young. Now I could probably do a decent job of that, though I'd definitely have to brush up on some grammar formalities and its seemingly obscurantist vocabulary. But after thinking about it, I decided that it just wasn't right for me. It wouldn't be an expression of my voice, like teaching a class on writing an essay or developing a character would be.

The tools are important indeed, but the authentic voice is transcendent.

Here's a good, helpful essay[3] on finding and developing your writer's voice, courtesy of Writer's Digest (and here's another fine one,[4] on the same topic from Jane Friedman). An important point in both essays is that the expression of self in writing, be it in diction, passion, slant or tone, can be a variant thing—the hummingbird's flight is always expressive of the bird, but its dartings and hoverings aren't always approached from the same direction or desire.

---

[3] http://www.writersdigest.com/whats-new/how-to-bring-your-voice-to-life-in-personal-essays

[4] http://janefriedman.com/2011/10/10/find-your-voice/

It's Not Stealing If You Honk and Wave, Is It?

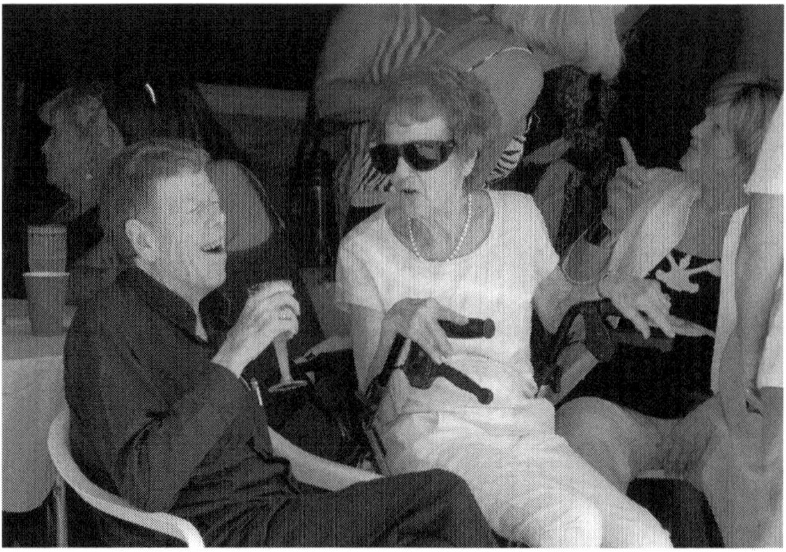

My mom getting the local priest tanked up on margaritas

What you read obviously influences your writing voice. Influences are a tricky thing. Of course I think you should steal freely the scent of another author's writing, that ungraspable soupçon of ephemera that is clumsily dubbed "style." That's because you'll catch your tongue in the literary rat trap if you try to directly steal the substance of another's writing. Mumbling out inane imitations will be your sorry fate. Snagging some stylings is more subtle theft, like being able to mimic the way an author buttons her coat, rather than actually buying—and eek!—wearing the same clothes.

Blood as Influence

But thinking of influences makes me think of other influences from way back: my parents. I have so much to be grateful for in having a mother who didn't harangue me and my siblings about reading as a necessity, but instead, took so much pleasure in reading herself. You'll develop a hunger for something in watching another eagerly eat it. There were always books around the house, and the relaxed sense that wiling away some hours nose-deep in a tome wasn't a way to waste time but to explore it: books are time travels, the widest carpets of brilliant flowers on the steppes, a landowner's cruel glance at the starveling slave, the wince from a princess as she turns her delicate ankle stepping from the liveried carriage.

My mother welcomingly invited me into that parlor of pleasant musings and savage astonishments, and I haven't looked back. From my earliest memories, I saw her absorbed in reading. Hey, books! They must be good. I want to do that too. She never pushed reading on me, but the obvious pleasure it afforded her was generously transferred to me. And because she could shape a story, could find the odd and often humorous angle on some episode of human folly, I was drawn to storytelling too. Before Sarge Bentley[5] got his hands on her, she was Eileen O'Brien, and though Iowa cornfields were the setting for her growing up, I'm sure the storytellers of the Old Sod made their ancestral mark on her. And she on me.

---

[5] http://www.tombentley.com/epitaph-writing/a-last-salute-to-the-sergeant/

Stories: 100% Nutritive, Taste Great Too

The absorbing thing is my mom's stories, like her life, have never been pocked with pettiness, or buzzing with the trivial, or interested in shoving someone aside so she could shine. As a writer, I tire myself with my own jealousies over other writers' successes, with my own trivialities and peeves. My mother has never swum in that shallow end of the pool—she laughs at the human comedy, but there's never been spite in her smiles.

So here's to my mom, my biggest writing influence. The photo is from her 90th birthday party a few years ago, where she was surrounded by friends, young and old, who uniformly wished her well. She's wearing those test-pilot's welding glasses because she can barely see a damn thing anymore and light bothers her, but she still reads wielding a fat magnifier. Words—can't get away from them. By her side is a priest from my old parish being entertained by her point of view (though the margarita he's drinking may have helped).

Thanks Mom.

My father wasn't a big reader, more inclined to the peppered nuggets of the newspaper than the seven-course meals of Russian novels, but again, I might never have been the reader, and thus the writer, that I am had he not schooled me in how to throw a baseball, how to shoot a basketball, things that impelled me to read biography after biography of my sports heroes (and to admire the tight turns-of-phrase of gifted sportswriters).

Always the Twain Shall Meet

Thinking about my less-genetic writing influences, I make a beeline for Mark Twain—why not set your standards high? But then I mentally mosey about some, bumping into Kurt Vonnegut, who seemed to pick flowers from the same field as Mr. Clemens. But whether a writer's echo can be heard in your work isn't necessarily a mark of their sway over you. There are people whose writing I fiercely admire, like Marilynne Robinson or Cormac McCarthy or Annie Dillard, and the DNA of their superb stylings can't be traced to my pratfalls on the page. (For that matter, I may have been influenced as much by Dr. Seuss, or maybe Steve Martin.)

In the intro to this book, I used "filling the table" as a metaphor for what the chapters contained. Going back to those influences, I'd toss a salad of Dillard and Atwood, a tangled pasta of Twain and Fitzgerald, spicy sides of Nabokov and Vonnegut, a shot of Cormac McCarthy, neat. But doesn't that sound a mite pretentious, as though I could even carry the keyboards of those authors (or even tilt Twain's first typesetting machine, one of his long legacy of infernal investments). And who's to say that I wasn't just as influenced by the comic books I devoured (I wanted to name a pet after Mjolnir, Thor's hammer), or the sports magazines that filled my mind with shimmering baseball diamonds and long fly balls caught after an impossible run?

Maybe I'm not being clear here, so let's clarify: your writing voice is a thing that develops over time, and that's touched, however subtly, by the roof over your childhood head, the flavors of everything you've read (and maybe even by what you've eaten—there's a lot of gluten in my writing voice). That voice is something that can be coaxed and coached. And it ain't static: your ability to refine, expand and improve your writing voice—and thus your writing—is a river in motion. Hopefully moving forward.

Why Writing What You Know Blows (Except ...)

Before I get a bit deeper into how to cultivate your writing voice, I have to take some exception to that hoary old adage of "write what you know." That dictum seems to suggest that you have to be deeply steeped in a subject to plumb its depths in writing. No. You just have to be careful in the research and in the writing. And sometimes you just have to let fly.

I was a teacher at a college on a small Micronesian island[6] for a year. One of my teaching duties was to attend college-related extracurricular events and presentations, which usually offered a wide range of foods. Micronesians are festive people: they like a good get-together, and they like to lard the table with a cornucopia of foodstuffs. At first, because I wasn't familiar with many island foods and how they looked after preparation, I would always be the slow one in line, peering closely at some dishes. Why? Because I didn't want to eat any servings of dog (and probably one that had tried to bite me while bicycling a few hours before the feast).

My dog-ducking wasn't because I truly *minded* that Rover had been barbecued—I've written before about the spirited chases

[6] http://www.tombentley.com/Micromacro.pdf

that mange-ridden canines[7] gave me on my bike rides, and the improvised weaponry and tactics used to dispatch those hounds of hell. It's just that the thought of eating dog unsettled me. In my culture, it's OK to eat a 1,200-calorie triple cheeseburger, containing enough salt to brine an Olympic pool. And in my youthful subculture, I spent an effortful afternoon making chocolate malts infused with ground peyote buttons.

But eating dog? No. Writing about eating dog? Oh my yes. I didn't have to chew any cur to chew over writing about the act.

The old "write what you know" adage blows in so many ways that I'll only enumerate a few: you often don't know what you know. Does that mean you can't write in a woman's voice if you're a man? Or you can't write about the 19th century because yours is the 21st? That aside, I do think some writers, fiction or non, essayists or poets, neglect to plumb their histories for the page-producing pools that they are.

I was out of my element in so many ways on that faraway island, but the combination of the odd and the exotic provided me with fodder for at least five published articles—most of which had to do with how I didn't know how to live on an island; not knowing (and puzzling over that ignorance) is fertile fodder. But let's also look at some of the ways that you can employ your earned experience on the keyboard.

---

[7] http://www.besttravelwriting.com/btw-blog/great-stories/second-annual-solas-awards-winners/travel-and-sports-silver-winner-going-to-and-away-from-the-dogs/

The Write Stuff: You Already Own It

In your own history, you've probably done a juicy fruit basket of unusual things. You've met people who have baffled you, intrigued you, offended your socks off. You've breathed sweet fragrant airs or shivered uncontrollably in climates not your own, you've worked for scowling bastards, you were given gratifying gifts that were wholly undeserved, you made decisions that a month prior you would have thought quite insane. You've lived.

Write about it. But in the writing, you will know those things in an entirely different way: you can push their emotional contents, stretch an image, color in a different corner: you are writing what you know, but not exactly—you are writing to know what you know, more deeply.

You don't even have to write about it directly—have one of your short story characters say those nasty things you itched to tell your pestiferous second cousin. Run through your memories, and some branches will catch your clothes. Just as I wrote that, I thought about my 13-year-old self, roaming the Long Beach Pike, that long-gone, fascinatingly seedy beachfront boardwalk—and doorway-watching in goggle-eyed compulsion as a woman in a tattoo parlor had her breast inked. Not having made any direct acquaintance of female breasts at that point, let's just say I was interested. That boy and his mesmerized look will end up in a story.

But it's not just lurid chapters in your childhood that make for the best source material—it's the trip you took to the tire dealership last month, where you noticed the grizzled old mechanic who clamped his jaw on an unlit cigar while he worked his tools. It's noticing that the H.R. head at your office has an oddly aggressive way of pointing with her index finger while she talks. Your mind is populated, spilling over, with pictures of people and places and things you looked at, touched, were repelled by. Write about them. Using the life-stuff of your times as the font of your writing is as satisfyingly savory as any dog sandwich.

You'll Be Surprised What You Know

Here's an example of the upside-down (i.e., unexpected) results of writing what you know. I once got an assignment in a writing group to write an "object" poem, using this overview: "Discuss how objects have lives and that they are often markers in our lives that help us recognize where we've been. They contain a special luminescence, connecting our past to our present."

Though I enjoy reading some poetry (Rilke, astonishing; Billy Collins, charming), I know very little of its formal structures, and know less about writing it. That said, it's a fun exercise to try writing out of your genre, so I thought I'd write an object poem about the humble sandwich. But instead, this came out, almost immediately after I started writing:

Sad Sandwich

Sad sandwich on the bedside tray
  moved in haste, forgotten in the empty house
  bedding thrown back in caught anxiety
  the last sandwich

Thousands of sandwiches before
handled with his child hands
then later, workingman eager, lunchpail eager
laughing with full mouth, laughing with work friends
then later, cold sandwiches in the bomber,
cold over Berlin, cold over Korea

Then, long past being able to make his own sandwich
my father's hands, delicate, veiny, persistent
still enjoying his sandwiches
but now all slowed, a slow sandwich, eaten contemplative

Thousands of sandwiches, thousands now forgotten
the one appearing on the daybed tray forgotten in a minute,
but still the slow pleasure of the chewing, the body's nod
yet, this last sandwich, a sad sandwich,
abandoned in the slant of afternoon light
my father, gone forever, this past New Year's Day
the plate now empty, the hunger unending

Writing That Surprises the Writer

This was one of those odd experiences as a writer, much as fiction writers say that their characters do things that surprise them as they're written. Here, I'd intended to write a light poem, and instead, it morphed under my fingers to be a tribute to my father, who died just a few months before that poem came to be. Without my even intending it, the poem became "... a special luminescence, connecting our past to our present."

So, an object poem, written with surprise tears. It always

amazes me, the weight of words. Speaking of writing with emotion, that is definitely a direct path to finding your voice. When you write where something is at stake—you were fired, your child was threatened by a bully, you parachuted out of a flaming plane—the charge of circumstance can bring electricity to your writing, and the pretenses of having to produce something formal or "literary" drop away.

But channeling emotion to drive your creative writing can be a two-way street: Writing fueled by emotion can pulse with the power of realness, show broken skin or broken heart; it's where you write from being *in* the game, rather than watching it. But writing from a personal current can also produce florid overwriting, work that's colored by mawkish hues, or even blindly inaccurate prose that freezes on a fixed point of view. I think focused, emotional writing can smack a ringing bell, but that misdirected emotion in writing can dilute its strengths, making it merely personal.

Here is an excerpt from some thoughts I wrote a long while back (about a year before my father's death), where I'm writing *about* writing with emotion (and in the writing, getting emotional, but am trying to direct the words for fullest impact, not melodrama):

I've written for publication about his condition prompted by an emergency room visit before,[8] *when his diminished capacity wasn't as advanced, but lately he's turned a corner, and even if his body lingers, his mind is becoming more ghostly, his world a small, small corner, with dimming light. I again want to write about my father, want to*

[8] http://www.youandmemagazine.com/articles/life-and-death-in-the-emergency-room

write again about how I never truly knew what he wanted, what his aspirations were, whether he judged his life a good one, if he even did pause to judge it.

Fathers and Sons, Arms Linked, Arm's Length

I've previously touched upon how my father's manner resembles mine in some ways: a person quick to make a joke, but in the joking also perhaps making a space between himself and others, perhaps more comfortable with a certain distance. I know that is true of myself, but I don't absolutely know if it's true of my father, because I never felt intimate enough with him to probe. I know he's always been a warm man, a reliable caretaker of my siblings and mom, a war veteran, a guy who taught me, to my great pleasure, to play baseball and basketball. But those are thrown-off evaluations, resume-writing; the core of the man is elusive to me.

So, my father, diapered, his country now a small bed, the tv on to keep him "company," attended by my valiant, near-blind mother, at 87, herself slowing to time's great watch. And I want to write about it, with emotion, but accurately, with the precision my father is entitled to, not to force anyone (or myself) to feel my discomfort, but just to write with the deserved passion that testifying about someone's life requires, without twisting the words to torque feelings.

Here's to writing that's real. It will have a rich voice; you need to shape it for its deepest resonance.

A Little Bit More About What You Know (or Only Know by Writing)

Since I'm the only one here right now with the keyboard to contradict (or at least circle around) myself, I want to circle around the "write what you know" dictum a little more, in regards to a writer's memory. I'll circle because it relates again to my father's death, so it's on topic here. Or at least it's in the same building.

A long time ago, I read an article where the writer suggested that Hemingway killed himself not because of his depression, but because of the treatment for his depression. The suggestion was that the electroshock had erased a good deal of Hemingway's memory, and that a writer without memories is not a writer—and that that loss provoked Hemingway's hand. However, much information has come out regarding his long-deteriorating mental and physical state prior to his suicide, and the loss-of-memory issue might have only played a minor part, if any.

The reason I bring that up is in thinking about when I went down to Southern California to spend some time with my mother, to honor what would have been my father's 94th birthday, his first birthday after his death. We went out to the graveside and saw the stone for the first time. My mother, in her natively collected and humorous way, remarked that it was a little odd to see her own name on the stone, which awaits what I hope is a long time to make claim to its inscription.

During the visit, my mother, sister and I shared memories of my father, a couple of which were new to me. That conversation in turn pushed me to rummage through my memory attic, blowing the dust off some crusted considerations of my boyhood long ago. It struck me that I hadn't made good use of some of the eccentric characters I've known over time, many of whom are easy subjects for the kind of tales that evoke a "No way! That couldn't have happened!" response from astonished or amused listeners.

Memories Are Writers' Clay

It's clear to me that most lives, whether you were raised in a dusty Ethiopian village of 100 souls or born to a gilded Manhattan penthouse, are suffused with character and incident that could fill books, if you selectively shaped the telling. And that working of the clay of character or incident needn't be exclusive to fiction's floor—the mad workings of the human animal are prime frameworks for engaging essays as well. (Note that libel issues can sometimes constrain a telling, though with the right makeup and hat, you can hide your pawn in plain sight on the narrative chessboard.)

I've seen enough peculiar and striking expression of the vagaries of our species to fill the memory banks—I'm going to start withdrawing some so the investment pays off. Poke around in your skull a bit, look at some old photographs, ask a relative about the time your great-aunt poured a drink on Maurice Chevalier's head at a dinner party. Memories are material from which writers weave and because their messages are so close, their expression of your writing voice will likely ring true.

I want to circle back again to another part of the circle: the capacity to be surprised, and to incorporate that into your writing. I used that object poem above about my father to suggest how your writing might unfold in startling ways, fully unplanned. Another angle (and one that can seed a writing voice) is to use a surprising incident as a writing prompt.

My office is a 1966 Airstream, something I'll write about directly later in this book. It's set on the edge of my girlfriend's and my property, in a semi-rural area in central California. The trailer is surrounded by fields on all sides, and when you look closely, there's always something going on. Looking closely is a habit that all writers should have.

A while back, a cousin of the fellow above flew into my neighbor's field. It's not that unusual to see herons in the general neighborhood—after all, I took the photo of this sharp-beaked beauty just a few miles from my house. But he was near a watercourse, where there are all kinds of wiggly things for him to eat. My neighbor's field is weedy, scraggly land where no fish worth its saltwater would venture. So, seeing the heron fly onto the property and strike one of those heraldic heron poses was noteworthy.

Any excuse to abandon my work, I scuttled over to the Airstream window nearest the bird to watch *him* work. If you've ever watched herons at play in the fields of creation, they're often pretty deliberate about their doings. They might neck-jut a few feet or so into some shallow water, and then fix that acute-angle head for minutes at a time, undoubtedly trying to come up with some heron haiku. This featherhead did his kind proud by freezing in place.

But then he chicken-footed forward toward our wire fence and started doing a fascinating bob and weave, his long neck shimmying from side to side, cobra-style, while he simultaneously ducked up and down. I thought for a moment that he was sick, and was about to collapse in the field. Not quite. On one of his swinging swayings, he shot that head forward to the base of the fence and came up with a big lizard in his beak. I didn't have time to even gasp before he flipped his head a bit and swallowed him whole.

Galvanizing Readers with Electric Characters

That moment was shocking and unexpected—I was agog. The bird sauntered out of sight of the Airstream—probably to see if there were any armadillos around to play poker with—and when I came out a few minutes later to check on him, he had vamoosed.

Now, you're going to think that I'm bending a stiff bird to make a point, but honestly, when my head had returned to my body after watching that lizard slurping, I immediately thought that the bird's behavior was a good illustration of an approach to working with characters in stories. You can give your reader a good clap on their forehead by making a character do something astonishing once in a while.

You have to be careful here: I'm not talking about having a character spontaneously speak Swahili when they were raised in Brooklyn. I'm referring to having a character do something that's possible (and that indeed might be integral to that character's nature), but that's not probable, that breaks boundaries. Something that expands the character's potential or place in the reader's imagination. That kind of developmental concussion can push a story, or shape it in new ways.

The Frogs Are Not What They Seem

The second nature lesson—and one that again relates to writing—is something I'd learned earlier, but was reminded of again because I heard a tree frog croaking after a recent storm. But that was just a soloist: in springtime every year, the frogs that do their philosophizing near our water garden start to do it more boisterously. And they are *loud.*

When I first heard this resonant chorus years ago, my city-boy background prompted me to think it was the loud-mouthing of some large toads, maybe even bullfrogs. I'd look all over the place for the source of the croak-storm, but I could never see the buggers. It took me many searches to finally spot one. No wonder: Pacific tree frogs, the wide-mouthed worthies that comprise this orchestra, are only a few centimeters long. But when they are soliloquizing about their romantic talents to any lady frogs in the vicinity, they give it their all. They are Danny DeVito with an aggressive hangover.

As with the heron, the frogs nudged me in a writerly direction as well: work with characters that aren't quite what they seem. You might have a scrawny, wiry guy who turns out to have extraordinary strength, or a reserved little sister who later turns out to wail skronking bebop sax in a secret band. Stick some herons and some tree frogs in your writing—it will give it a stronger pulse. And this isn't just for fiction: God knows that business writing could use a phrase that's on fire, or a trapdoor opening and swallowing up the beautiful bride. Wake the audience up.

Oh, you probably should stick a swallowed lizard in there every once in a while too; some characters turn out to be the eaten, not the eaters.

Any animals making mischief in your writer's mind?

I'll touch upon the writer's voice at other spots in the book, but I want to round out this focused (give me some latitude on that) attention on one other component of a writer's voice: its oddness. Writers are often a bit outside the line—and that's a good thing! The line is often something that's toed, but not by most writers. They'd just as soon skateboard over that line. I'll use the example of eccentric car design to put some wheels on a writer's engine.

I love old cars. I've probably owned 45 cars, and that's a tortured tale of love and leaks. I was at a vintage auto concours a couple of years ago, where there was an eyeball-scorching field of gleaming chariots, where the "oohs and ahhs" were many and involuntary. But then I saw this rig pictured above, a BMW Isetta with a teardrop trailer behind. The Isetta took more than 30 seconds to reach 31 mph, topping out at around 50. That the owner of this one had the peculiar cant of mind to hook up a tiny—but usable—trailer behind struck me with its whimsicality.

I don't know where the quote "Normality is what cuts off your sixth finger and your tail" comes from, but the Isetta is an exemplar of the quote's creed. Sometimes that sixth finger is the only one that can get a grip on an unusual idea, so it's a shame to cut it off.

I read a *New Yorker* article[9] about David Eagleman, a professor of neuroscience and of his work on how the brain conceives, interprets, and filters its sense of time. The article is wholly fascinating, but one of the tangents discussed in the piece was the "oddball effect," which at its essence posits that the brain reacts with great focus and avidity to things that are outside the standard pattern, pushing the norm or subverting it, so much so that time itself seems to be dilated as a result of the brain's attention.

Here's to the Oddballs

Though I don't even play a scientist on TV, I can't address the measures or implications of that phenomenon, so I'll just turn it to my purpose: The oddball effect is often a sensation of incredulity, mixed with delight. It's when you pull up next to a car at a stoplight and the driver is wearing a gorilla mask. Good God! Good writing often is fueled by the oddball effect.

So, like the Apple ad that saluted the crazy ones and the misfits, I want to salute the eccentric writers, who stroke and poke our brains. People like Tom Robbins, who never met a metaphor he couldn't bend around a shooting comet, or Oscar Wilde, who while studying at Oxford University, would walk through the streets with a lobster on a leash. Or Lord Byron, who when told at Cambridge he couldn't keep a dog in his room, discovered that there were no rules against bears. So he got one. (Note: Can we draw any conclusions about prestigious English academies and lunacy?)

---

[9] http://www.newyorker.com/magazine/2011/04/25/the-possibilian

Bertrand Russell said, "Orthodoxy is the death of intelligence." Here's to the guy that owned a truly oddball car, an Isetta, and thought, "A little trailer to go with it, that's the thing!" He probably would have put a bear in there too, if he'd thought about it long enough.

We'll touch (and listen for) writing voice again and again in the book, but right now, let's turn to another anatomical phenomenon: writing eyes. Writers need to see, both in their literal lives, and on the page. That vision can be transformative. Let's entertain some of the ways to open your writer's eyes and think like a writer. (Catchy, eh? Could make for a good book title.)

3

A Writer's Eyes Are Always Open

Writers are made, not born. Writers are born, not made. Writers are born without maids. Whichever nature/nurture boxing glove you decide to swing in that battle, I hold that there are some distinct methods to cultivate a writer's eye, and that those cultivations can result in sweet writerly fruits. (Please excuse that the last sentence mixed its metaphors with a waffle iron rather than a whisk.)

Photo by Peter Forster

Our lovely kitty image above is figuratively indicative of my intent: as a writer, you must always look at situations with your writer's eyes. [It's hard to see in this black-and-white rendering, but kitty above has a blue eye and a green eye.] But each eye must have a different focus, while still giving you a clear picture. Before I get into the wherefores of bicameral write-sight, let's underscore one fundamental: there are stories EVERYWHERE.

No matter if you're a poet, a journalist, a short-story scribe or a Tweetin' fool, stories saturate your day—they are in your neighbor's mail (don't look!), your boss's impatient gait, how your daughter wrapped your Mother's Day present, why coins feel cold, a bat's favorite breakfast, and maddening calls from AT&T about expanding your network offerings.

Stories Are Everywhere

Stories are not the province of the high and mighty movers and shakers; stories rest there too, but they are much the stuff of the commonplace, the cupboard, the errant gesture, the box left on the bus bench. You just need a writer's eyes to see them.

So back to those bicameral distinctions: You need what I like to call a crazy eye and a calm eye. One eye is your open-to-all experiences self, your id eye, and the other is objective, your superego eye. A small example (and in a larger sense, how stories lurk in everything): You see a brightly colored bird. Your crazy eye opens—is there a story there on how the male birds are most often the ones with the wild plumage? Maybe an article on who the Audubon of today might be, if such a specimen exists.

Branch out: think about your first flight on an airplane. Could one of your characters have an overwhelming aversion to flying on airplanes, so that a scene on one in which he breaks down is pivotal to a story? What did Leonardo da Vinci have in mind when he designed that prototype flying machine?[10]

Rely on Your Crazy Eye, Collect from Your Calm Eye

Let your crazy eye go crazy. Your crazy eye is a speculator, a dreamer, the one that swigs the moonshine even when the lip of the bottle is mossy. When your crazy eye whispers (which is quite a feat for an eye), listen.

---

[10] http://www.backtoclassics.com/gallery/leonardodavinci/flyingmachine/

But you also need your calm eye. That eye questions and discerns—where might there be a market for that story, what's the natural lead for the story, do I really want to write that story, is there even a story there? Both eyes are your friends, and both are necessary for seeing that there's a story in everything, but that that story shouldn't necessarily be written by you. But you never know unless you open your eyes to it. (Personally, I like the crazy eye—it will sometimes make a crumpled bag in the street appear to be a body, before your wise eye tells you no.)

Your third eye, of course, is your calm Buddha nature, the eye on the face you had before you were born. That eye judges not. (Though it likes strong shots of whiskey—oh, wait, that's somebody else I know.) Keep all your eyes open, and story ideas will flood your inner screening room. Some of those blended visions will find their merry way to the page.

Writers Say Wow!

I've always loved the "beginner's mind" Zen story:

A university professor went to visit a famous Zen master. While the master quietly served tea, the professor talked about Zen. The master poured the visitor's cup to the brim, and then kept pouring. The professor watched the overflowing cup until he could no longer restrain himself.

"It's overfull! No more will go in!" the professor blurted. "You are like this cup," the master replied, "How can I show you Zen unless you first empty your cup."

I'm as protective of my various opinions—on how crusty bread should be, how far to jut out your chin when denouncing the opposition party's political platform, why you should wear black because there isn't a darker color—as the next guy. I've gathered those opinions over time, worried over their posture, tried coloring their roots when they have gone a bit gray.

But having a stance, an answer and an opinion on everything can be damn tedious sometimes. Sometimes you just want to say "Wow! Now that's something!"

That's part of seeing with a writer's eyes: a feeling, a way of looking, that writers need; it's a valve opening in your imagination, it's dropping the opinion suitcases so you can sprint without the weight, it's room for the fresh taste of the tea.

Wow!

Words for the Plucking

Sometimes words themselves seem to be bright objects that can be plucked out of the air and strung together in serried ranks of complement and charm. Out of nothing, a paragraph that prances—or one that cries and bleeds. In those moments, it's less the affected pose of practiced art, but rather a kind of verbal husbandry, a farmer grateful for an unexpected crop. This isn't precious wordsmanship, it's grace—and I'm grateful when it occurs.

What I'm getting at is that at some times in the creative process, it's less a "me" than that "Wow!" I alluded to above. (Conversely, it's more often, "this writing is shit!"—but that's realistic, not wallowing.)

But perspective is king: there can be beauty in the way a bus driver weaves her route, how a seventh-grader whistles a made-up tune, where the making of a good sandwich is an artful act. Those moments of grace can be fleeting, but a good sandwich is forever. Well, until lunch.

Consider this:

> *"It is necessary to write, if the days are not to slip emptily by. How else, indeed, to clap the net over the butterfly of the moment? For the moment passes, it is forgotten; the mood is gone; life itself is gone. That is where the writer scores over his fellows: he catches the changes of his mind on the hop."*
> *— Vita Sackville-West*

Keep hopping, and snap a net on that nervous mind.

When Given the Gift of a Story, Take It

Here's another example of how you can find a story falling into your path: A while back, I attended the wedding of a friend's daughter. It was a lovely setting, in a bower warmed by the early fall sun of Northern California. Prior to the ceremony, all was going satisfactorily, with sighing grandmothers, scanty-skirted wardrobe malfunctions and many tuxedo tuggings. The groom, a hearty, open-faced lug I'd never met, joined the assembled bridesmaids and groomsmen at the head of the crowd. All turned to watch the bride's stately approach, and she joined the groom at the altar, presided over by the minister, a Jerry Garcia-lookalike who grinningly bid them to join hands.

That's when I noticed that the groom was weeping. He was holding his beloved's hands, and was gazing into her eyes, and the tears were streaming down. The minister voiced some of the standard wedding pleasantries, but all the while, our boy on center stage was crying, shaking a bit in the depth of his emotion. He had to pause many times in the recital of his vows, and had to mop his face with a handkerchief all the while.

I watched the bridesmaids, and as you might expect, a number of them were crying too, but I could see that a few of the groomsmen, hearty fellows all, were showing some reddened eyes as well. Even one of the commercial photographers, a woman, was crying. The display of the raw male emotion became even more interesting when I found out that the groom was a cop.

The Lift of the Odd Angle (Snatch Those Stories When They Surface)

The reason I'm making note of this is that as storytellers, life gives us gifts. All you have to do is open your eyes (if they're not too full of tears) and note them. Here you have a situation where something plays against type. A cop, a tough guy, openly weeping at his wedding. It turned out that most of the groomsmen were cops too, and they weren't hiding their own rising feeling. I'm sure you know that there's a lot of machismo in the fraternity of the boys-in-blue—group cries are probably not the norm.

For a writer, it's one of those moments that you store away (or if you're someone who gets right on it, damn you, you use it right away). You make a cop character who chokes up when he arrests a criminal, but is otherwise mister macho. Or maybe your cop character organizes a secret group of emotional policeman, the Crying Cops, for encounter-group support. Or maybe the cop is only emotional around beautiful blondes, like our bride. (There are worse problems, I suppose.)

What I'm getting at is that you should keep your notebook at the ready, and write down those moments—and your life is full of them, if you look—where something is a bit unconventional, or off-kilter, or puzzling. Even if those things only provide a secondary character or a subplot, they give texture to your stories, and provide sparks for ideas and angles.

And who knows? The next time you get pulled over, you might get a crying cop, and he won't be able to write out the ticket because his pad is so damp from the tears.

A Cup of Coffee for the Eyes

I hope I don't sound like I'm some kind of superhero idea chaser; I'm exhorting you to look with your writer's eyes whenever you can, because it's so easy to fall back into the habit of looking without seeing. I'm forever guilty, but when the veil does lift, again, wow!

I said earlier that my girlfriend and I live on a small piece of property in Central California, a few miles from the sea. Though only minutes from the freeway, our neighborhood is semi-rural, with many neighbors owning several acres of land. Our little bit of sod is about 1/3 of an acre, essentially surrounded by open fields. Over the winter and into the spring, the field grasses grow high, drying to reedy, golden weeds, sometimes five feet tall.

And then, on an appointed day, a couple of the locals get on their riding mowers, and do an all-day mow, crisscrossing the territory in loud, patterned swaths of removal. This happens in late spring, and how we see is different: it's like wearing welding glasses and having them fall off. Look, a cat, fixed but quivering, paws flexed in front of the gopher hole! A covey of quail, their topknots bobbing, busy harvesting seeds. And how did we not know that under the waving weeds, a clump of calla lilies stand shining?

Writer's Slump

Writers are observers, but even observers fall into unseeing slumps. The buzzing of the hours, lunch followed by dinner, thoughts hovering on subjects well worn by prior thinking. You don't actually see your work, your girlfriend, your very self. There's a surface, and then there's what's underneath. What's underneath is often new, bright and fresh—but that freshness is actually there all along. If you only tilt your head rather than hold it straight, not hold it expecting today's fields to be the same as yesterday's.

Too many times I feel trapped in my mind, touchy, pessimistic, my thinking circular and petty. I've felt jealous of other people's success, doubting my own path, my mind small and cramped. But sometimes—like now—the walkway to my Airstream office is lined with bright poppies, supple stems swaying in the wind and gabbling goldfinches merrily dunk themselves in the deck-side water garden. The flowers are impossibly bright.

Spring is a state of mind as well as a season. Time again to see like a writer, see underneath the surface, to mow down the weeds of the small mind. Breathe. And when a writer's eyes are at their widest, it's always spring.

PS When your writer's eyes close, and you're all wrapped up in your small, sour self like I've been at times, it's good to read something like Leo Babauta's *38 Lessons I Learned in 38 Years.*[11]

Pick Your Writer's Plums

Speaking again of our rural property, for the last six or seven years, I've thought the withered plum tree in our yard was a goner. The tree would produce another season's worth of sweet, juicy fruit, and in the picking, I'd see the deep, dry cracks in the boughs. And the trunk: if you give it a good thump you hear a resonant return like a bass drum. It's at least half-hollow, rotted out—that its core is half-empty seems the loudest beat of the old tree's death knell.

How could it keep producing when its heart seems cracked? It's an old tree, at least 40, maybe even 50 years old. It suffered deep indignity the last couple of years after I stapled a rubber mat over the biggest of the trunk holes, where a big bough was lopped off before our time here, developing into a decaying maw that winter rains only worsened. Yet, for all that, for all its wear, its visible weight of age, its craggy twisted lines, in spring we have the

[11] http://zenhabits.net/38/

crown of blossoms, we have the thrill of seeing the green plums beginning to ripen, we have the bright explosions of pleasure from biting into their red ripeness.

Tree Twisted Into a Metaphor for Writing

I'll go out on one of those cracked limbs and twist this into a writing metaphor: when I finished the last harvest of plums this past fall, it made me think of how many times I've felt deficient, deformed or hollow as a writer, how I've felt that the trunk was cracked, the flowers few. But lately, even though there are more cracks than ever, I'm producing more, and the production is better, sweeter. I'm trying not to hold back any more, because I'm not sure how many plums there are to come.

So, I look at that old tree: It sings of its past, its plums to come, its plums now. Makes me think of Silverstein's The Giving Tree,[12] though I don't think I could get much in the way of a boat out of its sere limbs. But in the sense of the tree saying, "This is what I have. It's yours. Take it."

We should to do that with writing as well. What better way to round out thoughts about plums than with two of my favorite William Carlos Williams poems, both plummy:

This is Just to Say
I have eaten
the plums
that were in

---

[12] http://en.wikipedia.org/wiki/The_Giving_Tree

the icebox

and which
you were probably
saving
for breakfast

Forgive me
they were delicious
so sweet
and so cold

And this:

To a Poor Old Woman
munching a plum on
the street a paper bag
of them in her hand

They taste good to her
They taste good
to her. They taste
good to her

You can see it by
the way she gives herself
to the one half
sucked out in her hand

Comforted
a solace of ripe plums

seeming to fill the air
They taste good to her

So, bite the plums, write the words.

Letting the Bobcat Loose in Your Writing

I'm going to continue sticking in my own backyard for a bit, writing what I know about what I know. As I said, I live in a semi-rural area. My neighborhood is surrounded by stretches of tangled brush and stands of tall trees. There's a nice walk on a paved road through my neighborhood, and though there are many houses around, the road winds up and down some small hills, flanked by these areas of bushy scrub, scruffy oaks and fairly big pines.

There's also a bobcat. Or perhaps more than one, as you'll read below. The first time my girlfriend and I saw her on our walk, she was a distance away in a clearing, and I thought it was just a big house cat. But I could see the rumpy way she walked through some high weeds, and then could see the wispy flares on her ears. A bobcat! A wild thing, in context. Seeing an unexpected bobcat focuses the attention, stokes the heart, makes you tilt your head and consider things from a different perspective.

I advocate putting a bobcat in your writing. There's not a recipe for what I'm pushing, no "use two action verbs, vary sentence length and strangle the adjectives." No, instead I'm saying look for the places in your writing, whether it's business writing or the novel that has been drinking too much decaf—and put in a bobcat. Don't settle for the common phrase, don't settle for rote description, don't have your characters or your concepts always be tight and linear.

Whether it's with poetic language, an artful dodge, a right turn when a left was called for, a bright balloon in a sea of grey, a bobcat in your writing is a joyful thing. Look for the fields—or the corporate boardroom—where you can place one, and see what happens.

Naturally, you can't put a bobcat in every paragraph. That would de-claw it. No, find the places where it can pounce, and proceed.

Mors Pulchra

Mors Pulchra is Latin for "beautiful death." I bring that up because there was (and I hope still is) more than one bobcat in our neighborhood. I know that because once on one of our walks, we found one dead, very close to the road. Perhaps he'd been hit by a car, though there were no obvious signs of what had killed him. He was a strikingly beautiful animal, muscular, with a thick, tawny striped coat and surprisingly large paws. I felt a sense of loss and regret that was oddly touching.

Some writers are able to capture an essence of longing and "what might have been" in a way that isn't cloying or sentimental, and they can put it to use in their work. I had that emotional feeling when I looked at that bobcat, thinking that those big paws had scrambled up these hills in a swift flash of electric life.

It's a tricky thing to pull off, but there are also times when you want to put a *dead* bobcat in your writing. Done well, it can grab readers in a place where their brains don't call the shots.

So, bobcats as writing aids—who woulda thunk it?

The Writing Grind Can Grind You Down—Surface Through Another Writer's Words

Of course, sometimes there ain't no bobcats anywhere—just you and a page so blank it looks like its emptiness will swallow you whole. Could be you need another writer's take on the writing life. I've been rereading Annie Dillard's fine *Pilgrim at Tinker Creek,*[13] for the third or fourth time. It's a marvelous work, almost like drinking in the molten stuff of imagination itself, for the language of the book is a series of fireworks, pinwheels of whirling thought, cascades of explosive insight, and then soft candles of introspection.

Dillard gets her nose right into nature, flopping face down on the ground and opening her eyes wide and—with her alchemy of observation forged into words—tells us what she sees and how to see it, in a way that makes pages breathe. Among the many things that struck me in this reading was a passage about how cicadas go about their business:

"In the South, the periodical cicada has a breeding cycle of thirteen years, instead of seventeen years in the North. That a live creature spends thirteen consecutive years scrabbling around in the root systems of trees in the dark and damp – thirteen years! – is amply boggling for me. Four more years – or four less – wouldn't alter the picture a jot. In the dark of an April night the nymphs emerge, all at once, as many

---

[13] http://www.amazon.com/Pilgrim-Tinker-Creek-Annie-Dillard/dp/0060953020

as eighty-four of them digging into the air from every square foot of ground. They inch up trees and bushes, shed their skin, and begin that hollow, shrill grind that lasts all summer."

Now, that passage is much less poetic than countless others in the book, but the thought of those burly insects biding their time, working the years, establishing and refining all things cicada threw me into considering how long as writers we might be buried, mere potential, waiting for wings to harden.

It's always amusing when there's a new writing sensation, some breakout author who's touted as the newly crowned best and brightest, and you learn that they also have three other novels that never made a stir, and four that they abandoned or are still gestating. Loud (and potentially annoying) as those cicadas might be, they earned their shrill grind. The long seasons of work are often invisible to outside eyes, buried to all except the worker.

Words Have Sound, as Well as Shape and Sense

Sometimes writing work is a shrill grind. A while back, I read my unpublished novel aloud, *again,* in order to hear the rhythm of the words, to see if the sentences made music. I'd already edited it on screen, but putting voice to the page let me hear the places where the saxophone squawked rather than soared. In the space of twenty-five pages, I made at least seventy-five corrections, sometimes just transposing two words, sometimes shifting a phrase from sentence middle to end. It reminded me of when I've been given something to edit by a writer who thinks it's near done, and I return it to them dripping the blood of the red pen—the horror!

I'm going to give the novel another going over again soon—a bit tedious, but it's cicada work: something buried will burst forth. I'll be happy if the damn thing crawls, much less takes wing.

Let's end this thought with another passage from Dillard's work, this time from another book I highly recommend, *The Writing Life:*[14]

"One of the few things I know about writing is this: spend it all, shoot it, play it, lose it, all, right away, every time. Do not hoard what seems good for a later place in the book, or for another book; give it, give it all, give it now. ... Something more will arise for later, something better. These things fill from behind, from beneath, like well water. Similarly the impulse to keep to yourself what you have learned is not only shameful, it is destructive. Anything you do not give freely and abundantly becomes lost to you. You open your safe and find ashes."

Open your safes, writers. Whether you let the silver lie thirteen years or seventeen, you must let it go. Otherwise, it will tarnish. (Besides, you might be able to make the latest sale on quill pens at Walmart.)

When the Grind Seems to Hit the Soul

Speaking of the grind that writers sometimes feel, perhaps because I ate too many Snickers Bars as a child, since adolescence I've been set upon by bouts of existential dread. It harkens to Sartre's dark work, *Nausea,*[15] when even everyday objects—the

---

[14] http://www.amazon.com/Writing-Life-Annie-Dillard/dp/0060919884

[15] http://en.wikipedia.org/wiki/Nausea_(novel)

lamp, your keyboard, your wife—appear sinister and threatening. Is it true? Oh, absolutely, everything has its dark side. But you must outwit them: don't stare the mad dog straight in the eye, but give it a sidelong glance as you skirt its sharp teeth. After a while, the lamp goes back to looking like a lamp. Your wife might be more dicey.

I have an inner voice that often tells me I'm a horse's ass. Though that yoke occasionally fits, much of the time, it's just the little voice of habit and self-doubt. As most asses need slapping, I'll step to a mirror, look at the ass looking back at me and say, "You're just a horse's ass in the mirror, not my real self. My real self is a combination of Gandalf, Mother Teresa and Jimmy Kimmel. Begone!"

There are a lot of open fields in my neighborhood, where coyotes sometimes roam. I like to think of the mind, with its fears, hesitations and plunges, as a creature—like a coyote. Sometimes I see the coyotes slinking around, cur-like, with a guilty look. Other times I see them racing across the fields, and hear the merry yip-yip-yipping in the evening. I like to think of my coyote mind in this way: when it's slinking and guilty, it's but a small turn in perspective to release that mind. Release it to become the version of the Trickster that is both cunning and kind. That coyote brain yips its joy, not its fear.

Shakespeare, Faulkner, Austen all had days in which what they wrote was dung. On those days, they went fishing. So, whether in a bassy lake or a lake only of your imagination, drop a long line. Think of nothing. Feel the sun on your hands, the breeze on your forehead. The work will be there waiting for you, so bob that merry line until due time.

Laugh often, laugh loud. The world is a preposterous place, of pratfalls and puzzlements, where you go to scratch your nose and put your finger in your eye, where governments bloviate, where your neighbor wears his wife's bra (not that there's anything wrong with that), where the day you wax your car for the first time in a year, it rains.

You can't really account for the surreal, the stifling, the boring aspects of life. But this is the life you have—seize it, lick its neck, raise it skyward. The stories about the Other Place in the afterlife are just like filling an inside straight to me: possible, but not likely. So, it's this world, this NOW, that has so many tears in it—sometimes all you can do is laugh.

A writer's life is a peculiar one, of crooked gratifications and queer slights. So much is interior, subject to the fickle tastes and electrical storms of your own mind, which though you've sat in the room with it all your life, remains a mystery. Some days you might sling 1,000 good words over your shoulder, and shrug at its meaninglessness. Some days a single sentence will shine, and that's enough.

The hell with it—once in a while, choose to eat as much ice cream as you want.

What Happens When the Voice Is Strangled?

A particular kind of grind that most writers know is when the words just don't come. A disease variant for me can sometimes be, "Writer's Pathetic, Strangled Bleat of Knowing That I'll Never, Ever Write Anything of Consequence Again, Sob!" (Of course, that presupposes that you've already written something of consequence.) I'm a master of dithering when I'm beginning a writing project, searching desperately for nits to pick up off the floor, needing just another cup of coffee to add to the seven previous, accidentally browsing a Tahiti travel site for 45 minutes and on. But something always kicks in when I get that first paragraph done, so in scooping out the first shovelfuls, I wondrously often see the road being built.

Thus one of the first things to do is get your first paragraph written, no matter if it's for a 500-page novel or a 500-word blog post. A lead paragraph (or perhaps even a paragraph deep within the belly of the beast) can lead to a second, and a giddy third. I have seen repeatedly that a spark can touch off a fire. But there are things that can lead up to that lead, a setting of the writing table, a gesture to welcome the Muse in, a curt gesture to escort the idealess bum in the hammock out.

The external things that seem to help for me are exercising, reading something that's greatly unlike what I'm trying to write (perhaps sewing pattern books), or doing something that's mindless but physical, like rearranging my nun puppets. Exercising is really a good one for me: I get full sentences that honestly just jump into my head, particularly when I'm bike riding, so the sentences do get bounced around a bit before they get home.

The freelancer can choose from a mere umpty-trillion unusual Internet suggestions on how to stay healthy while working at home: wear Yoga Toes on your hands, drink smoothies made of blended artichoke hearts and pages from pocket dictionaries, only drink coffee from those famed beans that have been pooped out by civet cats. (Anybody ever try those? Still married?) And of course there are suggestions from the minds of middlebrow moderates, advocates of the standard soporific: eat sensibly and get good exercise.

But neither the fringe nor the fair-to-middlings catch the bottled lightning of exercising for the creative spark. I'm not talking about how 10 downward dogs a day might keep you in good enough shape to type another 200 words on your to-do list for 2017. I'm talking about how exercising can open your skull so that ideas pour directly in, and what was a stone soup becomes nourishment for your noodle, and spicily stirred.

Here's my recipe: have a writing problem. As a writer, you have writing problems. If you're a home-based knitter, you have knitting problems. If you're a coder, you have coding problems. The world is cruel that way. So, my writing problems are often of this nature: There are no words to say what I have to say. I'm doomed! (Cue sound of grown man bleating like a wounded lamb.) Here's a typical situation from a few months back: I had no angle on a magazine article I was writing, because the base material was abstruse, and I couldn't find a way in. The second was that I was stuck in a scene of the novel I was writing, and it was a scene needful of a narrative explosion.

How Pedaling Your Bike Is Pedaling Your Mind

I took my standard approach to solving this problem: I found some dust on the rear of my monitor, and I blew it off. I went in the house and ate a handful of peanuts. I checked Google News to see if Ted Cruz was advocating arming grandmothers with hand grenades so they are safe while shopping. Surprisingly, my writing problems weren't solved. But then I did something that has worked so many times before, and because I have banana peels where rational thought should be, something I always forget: I went bicycling.

But I didn't go bicycling to furiously pedal while I furiously considered my writing problem. You see, I'd already done that while I was working with dust, peanuts and Ted's grenades. Professorial braniacs have discovered that when you prime the pump of the mind, putting some pressure on that extraordinary neuronal glob within your noggin, it will seem to work out the primed problems on its own, without your direct intervention. In fact, in my case, it's always better to stay out of the way.

Cut to bike—while I moved merrily along the Santa Cruz coast, thinking that it's so wonderful how climate change had me in shorts and a t-shirt in February and wondering if that means the next Ice Age will start in June, my brain sent me an instant message: problems solved. In succession, I heard in my brain the full, word-for-word title of the magazine article I wanted to write, and that title gave me the angle into the material.

Next, the solution to my slagging scene in the novel, complete with several phrases I could use verbatim and a full sentence that set the scene's full stage. Business-writing problem solved, pleasure-writing problem solved. And I did not crash the bike.

But I did marvel. It occurred to me again, duh, that if you have your clammy hands around the neck of your mind while trying to extract a concept confession, relaxing your hands will let the confession come out. This has happened to me many, many times, often while biking, sometimes while hiking, and once in a while picking nits off of the floor. (Note: you can buy bags of nits at the Nit Store if you don't have any around the house.) Maybe you can do it golfing, shooting skeet, or popping your head back and forth over the neighbor's fence to see if there's any sunbathing going on.

So, whatever the cognitive mechanism by which this works, it does work. So whether you are avidly exercising so that you'll be a bite of buff cake for your sweetheart, or you find the whole notion of working up a sweat too much work, consider that it's actually a way to receive useful gifts from the cosmos. The cosmos is a giver of gifts—just move into a position to catch them.

Grab That Fluttering Idea (But Don't Strangle It)

Following that thought: grab the idea while it flutters, because it will only be loose feathers when you come back to it later. If you get a sentence in your mind without writing tools available, keep writing it in your mind. Not only will the idea be refined, but it will stick long enough to remember it, or at least its essence. This is the method I most often practice on the bike.

It's worth noting that often periods that seem the most frustrating, when you're PLEADING with your brain to muster up something your character needs to say, and all you get is the stone wall of silence, relax: that wrestling match often results later in the sought-after medal. So often I've looked at the mute letters of my keyboard, given up and gone on to make a sandwich, and while spreading the mustard, I hear the "pop" in my head. Ideas need to incubate, to fledge, dear little birds that they are.

You could also keep one of those small digital recorders close at hand, if mental notes turn to mist for you. And of course, the old reporter's notepad is a mainstay—I just used one on a recent travel assignment for the *LA Times* and though my scrawled notes while hiking up at Pinnacles National Park were more twisty than the trails, I was still able to salvage some copy out of my cacography. (My camera does have a function to record audio notes with every photograph, but I always forget to use it.)

A 90-Proof Shot of Inspiration

But truly, if you can empty the glass right when inspiration pours you a shot, do it. Too often I've tossed and turned over an article idea at night, come up with an angel-winged solution there in bed, and then not written it down. Angel wings turned to broken bones overnight—the actual words, which for me are the batteries of the idea, are often lost. I always get up and write ideas now, even if Morpheus is pulling me back down.

Let your great ideas get thrown into the pit of dreams, and they will emerge as dead skin and dross.

I'll leave with the biggest way to chip that monolithic writer's block: a slice at a time. Particularly for a long-distance swim like a novel, it's easy to think you'd never get 400 pages down, and thus, it's easy to quit. But giving yourself a narrow, easily achievable goal—writing 15 minutes a day—and that Atlantic swim becomes a few breast strokes through the pool. You might have so much fun in your 15 minutes, you could even go for 20.

Oceans are crossed by the steady swimmers.

Trippin' into the Keyboard

One of my favorite ways to open the writer's spigot is to travel. Traveling to somewhere you've never been, especially when you stay for more than a few days, exerts odd temporal and spatial pressures on your consciousness. That Heraclitus quote about never being able to step twice in the same river is of a piece with what I'm talking about: your traveled self is not the same self untraveled. And extending upon that, the "home" you return to seems a little slippery too: after travel, I keep glancing around here like there's a joke being played, like the walls of the house are hastily thrown-up curtains with a corner out of plumb. But that kind of feeling "a bit off" is fertile ground for writing.

In the last couple of years, my gal Alice and I have spent some stints outside the US: a couple of months in the Bahamas a couple of years ago, later a month in Panama, and seven weeks in San Miguel de Allende, Mexico most recently (and maybe Hawaii again this fall—the glories of house-sitting). Among all the things that bit me in those thermal zones must have been an unbalance bug, because my thinking has been just a wee bit off since then. Nothing major: just the usual "Is the life I'm living real or just a series of disconnected contingencies?"

If This Life Isn't Real, Would You Mind Adjusting the Sound Track?

Rack one up for the contingency corner. It's not that I've ever doubted that our scraping skating on this little ice chip of a planet was held together by hand-tightened screws (and punctuated by pratfalls and whoopee-cushion sounds), but going and living in other cultures, even insulated by the knowledge that you'll return to your own, is oddly jarring. Or maybe it's just that the literal jarring of crashing my Panamanian host's car into a high-grass-concealed curb and smashing the front suspension while visiting there torqued my steaming cranium a mite.

To the point (god, man, finally—this ramble is wearing on me): I've begun to write some of the literal (and some merely mental) adventures that took place overseas, out of my alleged comfort zones, because if I continue to wait, I fear that whatever lies and distortions I do distill in that writing might not bear even a shadowy relationship to fact. The fish-out-of-water story—when the gaspings of the fish are sharply rendered—can still provoke interest. It's just odd to come back and have the water at home taste just a little weird.

Kate probably base jumps too

A Writer's Attitude Should Be a Little Punk

I love this photo of Kate Hepburn. Even though her both-feet-athwart stance seems to presage a butt-tumble to come, the fact that she's cranking the angle shows she's not just rolling a flat-foot-dead-ahead-I'm-terrified skate, but she's going for it. Maybe it's the only time Kate skated, maybe it's just a publicity photo, but implicit in it is the kind of attitude confirmed by Hepburn's biography: a brash kind of what-the-hell brio that was disarming and refreshing.

That's what I think writers should do: push the angle a little, crank off some language that's bolder or brighter, be willing to take a bone bruise to your writer's elbows. I like to imagine Kate grinding on a curb in the Safeway parking lot, the security guard saying, "Hey lady, give it a rest!" From reading of her history, she rarely gave it a rest: she was opinionated, strong-willed and emotional, and it came out in her acting and her personal life. Whether you write for business, pleasure or both, writing doesn't have any flavor unless you add some cayenne now and then.

The Long Hangover from a Word-Bender

When I was ten or eleven, I became slaphappy with words. I'd read the dictionary in chunks of pages, getting into the brief etymologies, mouthing the pronunciations. I remember running down to my best friend's house, having memorized a line about a nice, old Volkswagen bus his highly educated parents had bought, so that I could spring on them something like "Congratulations on purchasing a well-restored vintage mode of transportation," or some such gobbledygook. My friend's dad just looked at me and laughed, though in a kindly way.

Despite regularly getting those kind of skeptical responses, I continued being a word-dweeb for years. The editor of my college paper was a guy who liked me and my writing, but one who accurately judged that my polysyllables-per-sentence count was choking many readers. He once titled an article of mine about an unconventional housing design near the college, "A Lot of Big Words About Housing."

I've calmed down some from those days. I'm no longer so insecure about my writing that I have to forcibly lard it with fifty-cent words to make it seem worth something. But I'm still thrilled by language, still rifling through the dictionary, still wanting to goose a sentence with word-grease that makes it jump. So, take some chances with your writing: think of Kate Hepburn shredding in a half-pipe, no kneepads.

Bonus Celebrity "No Way!" Sighting

This might not seem to obviously relate to writing voice, but it's at least in the same house—at least in the house where on the top floor the writer sings opera too. Agatha Christie was a surfer.[16] I knew that Mark Twain did it in Hawaii (look for his tales of "surf bathing" in the Sandwich Islands), but Dame Agatha? Yes! I am hoping that one of you can find out whether Yogi Berra was a knitter.

---

[16] http://www.guardian.co.uk/books/2011/jul/29/agatha-christie-hercule-poirot-surfing-secret

You Don't Need the Cigars for Writing Contemplation (But I Might)

I think part of your attitude should be expressed in your habits, whether directly connected to writing or not. For instance, one of my favorite Sunday afternoon pastimes (ahh, "Sunday pastimes," which smacks of a gentler era seen through a bit of a mist) is smoking a fat cigar and reading the newspaper, parked in a chair in my garage, which looks down our long driveway to the strawberry fields beyond. For me, the hour or so I spend, perhaps a couple of Sundays a month, is one of those concentratedly "small" respites, where I breathe (really, despite the smoke), reflect on the triumphs and tribulations yodeling from the newsprint, and often consider a writing problem or possibility.

There are long beds the length of the driveway host to a mélange of flowering plants, shrubs and trees, so the humming of the hummingbirds and the bumbling of the bees provides a palette of color and pleasant movement, where I drink in droughts of pastoral pleasure in between recoiling from the accounts of the latest global atrocity, or wagging my head at some pundit's proclamations.

That smoky solace might let me take a sharp turn on an essay I've been writing in my mind, something which to that point had been a tangled skein of thoughts without warp or woof. There's something about sitting in a hazy repose that's of value to a writer, when the mind's hummingbird dips into enough flowers to secure a sweet idea. Of course, the real trick is to implement, to actually weave something from the woolgathering. So I try to make it a habit, when I've been gifted with something more than fragrant breath from my cigarish contemplations, to get to the keyboard lickety-split, and weigh and record the nugget from the Sunday pannings. As I alluded to earlier, jumpy writing ideas will turn to fool's gold if you don't stick a pin in them.

Kindling Your Writing

But it also occurred to me that "man in driveway with cigar and newspaper" is an anachronism, a diorama of a soon-to-be-bygone scene, with the newspaper now so much thinner than my cigars, and smoking in itself an odious step on the slippery slope to child pornography and wearing Crocs in church. I suppose I could read Elizabeth Barrett Browning on the Kindle while I drink some herb tea, but that doesn't supply the requisite amount of vice for my tastes.

Besides, I take comfort in the rustle of the newspaper, the ever-morphing patterns of the rising and dissipating smoke, the acid balance of the big cup o'joe that's always part of the picture. (When that cuppa isn't the occasional brandy, the drinking of which is just another notch on St. Peter's staff, so that when I arrive at the pearly gates, he says, "You're kidding, right?" But don't forget that Mrs. Browning did like a swallow of opium or two in the middle of all that poesy*.)

Of course, my particular prescription to invite the writing muse might not be for everyone. Quilting might substitute well for the newspaper, but then you might light your handiwork on fire with the cigar ash. (And for women worried that those stubby sticks will clash with their gold lamé gowns, really, there are some slender panatela and cigarillo-style stogies that lend themselves just as well as those fulsome fatties to stylish, airy gestures and erudite commentary.)

But I think every writer should have a retreat, a place of studied measure and sifting, a place where you become The Thinker, only without the weight of all that bronze. A writer's retreat, whether physical or philosophical, anachronism or not, is a yeasty place of stirring idea. Consider Virginia Woolf's *A Room of One's Own,*[17] and apply it to your state. And be sure to wash the ashtrays afterwards.

*PS If you want to get a hint of writer vices gone to polysyllabic extremes, read *The Confessions of An English Opium Eater,*[18] by Thomas De Quincey. It is a word-drenched testimony of the drug's effect on his senses and his writing, and is worth at least scanning for the cascade of voluptuous compound sentences and twirling literary merry-go-rounds.

Sometimes Storytellers Don't Even Need Words

A long while back, on a very atypical spring day, I had one of those peculiar writing revelations about how stories and writing voices are shaped. There were thrashing rain squalls, gusty, spiraling winds, and wet, wet, wet. I ran around town doing errands, hunched and squinting in the ancient Benz I drove at the time, windows fogged, because the heater blower has given up the ghost. But there was a short break in the rain, so I drove over to Steamer Lane, one of California's premier surf spots, to look

[17] http://www.amazon.com/Room-Ones-Own-Annotated/dp/0156030411/

[18] http://en.wikipedia.org/wiki/Confessions_of_an_English_Opium-Eater

at the crashing waves. Too blown out for surfers that day, but there were a couple of kiteboarders whipping across the scudding waves, digging the wild winds.

It occurred to me that the boarders were writing on the waves, kind of free writing, where you don't pause to reflect on the course of the narrative, but you just let the pen roll, the words barreling through willy-nilly, one word trampolining higher than the next, or slipping its nose under the surface of those to come. It's a kind of writing I don't often do, being the prim walker of my writing dog, usually leashed.

How Do You Tell Stories Without Words?

But the rollicking kiteboarders had me thinking further—it being a rainy day and all, perfect for damp musing—what would it be like to tell your stories without words? They were writing stories on the waves, stories of exuberance and thrill, of experiment and error (and recovery from error), of sheer, spontaneous spunk. There are so many different ways of telling stories, but writers think—and write—in words.

Language has always come easily to me, probably because I loved the play of words from childhood. Since my young punk days, I thought being a writer, a storyteller, was an exalted vocation. Because I couldn't hit a curve ball (professional ballplayer being my first dream), I chose the curve of words. Now that I'm an old punk, I still think of writing as one of the best approaches to map out your world. But considering how few people work with words on an intimate basis, I wondered if many people, particularly today (where word-worthiness doesn't seem a premium), perceive not owning the bricks to build up a story structure as an insufficiency or a frustration. But maybe their stories are wrought from different iron.

Lone Cowboy

There are many kinds of storytellers, of course. As I alluded to before, years ago I was held in thrall by a crusty old mechanic who, chewing vigorously on an unlit cheap cigar and spitting into the engine recesses of our disabled '55 Chevy, rattled out a sequence of profane tales. A born word-worker, spouting stories in a dilapidated old gas station at a dusty crossroads out of Wasco, California. He certainly didn't need any paper (and maybe didn't even need an audience).

When you look closely, you can see storytelling everywhere, often wordless; the barista at your local coffee shop might make a perfect cappuccino with a swift succession of rhythmic motions, each musically timed, so that a once-empty cup is filled not with coffee but a warm poem.

Approximately a thousand years ago, I hitchhiked across Canada with my best friend. In one of the little towns we were stuck in, we went to a local park and watched a Little League baseball game in some rickety bleachers. While we were sitting there, we were accosted by a skinny, scruffy old man wearing a droopy cowboy hat and carrying a harmonica. When he asked "Could I play a song for you today?" there was no answer but yes. He got up close to the both of us, and played a series of short songs, none of which I recognized. His face, lined, tired, told a story that didn't need any musical accompaniment. When he was finished, we thanked him, and he said, "I'm the Lone Cowboy, you know." He started to leave and turned back, and with a big, rheumy-eyed grin said, "I kissed a pretty girl today. I'm the Lone Cowboy!"

The delighted, crafty and slightly self-astonished look in his eyes told as much of a story as his words. Here's to the crusty mechanics, slick-serving baristas and Lone Cowboys, storytellers all.

Hearing Through a Writer's Ears

My dad, pajama-party king

Let's shut the writer's eyes for a spell and listen up: A common piece of advice for novel writers is to create character backgrounds for all of the main figures in the work, most often prior to beginning the writing. Those backgrounds could be considerable: you might detail not only the characters' general physical appearance and temperament, but things like what cereal he regularly eats (and if he slurps the bowl), her favorite kind of weekend dance music, which of their grandparents had thick hair, which the boldest gestures.

The concept behind this is that although—and even *because*—few of these minor details will ever be employed in the plot, you will have so saturated yourself in your characters' consciousness that their actions as the story unfolds are direct reflections of the fullness (and often eccentricity) of their personalities.

The Sound of Memory

I was thinking of those things because I'd been trying to clearly remember my father's laugh. That shouldn't be too hard: my father lived 93 years, and he laughed easily, and enjoyed the laughter of others. Most of the photographs of my father show him with a broad smile, even after his Alzheimer's robbed him of the clarity of his concerns. But I've had some trouble remembering the exact tone of my father's laugh, its timbre, how it might build or fade.

That alarmed me, because my father has only been dead a few years. But my efforts were rewarded, because I was able to finally pull from memory the quality of his chuckle, how his face shaped his mirth and vice versa, and how the general atmosphere was lifted by the lilt of his laugh.

My struggles illustrate a useful writer's lesson: pay attention to the details in your day-to-day—all of them. Fix them in your memory. It's that airy wave of your first lover you don't want to forget, because one of your characters might need that wave to fully become flesh in your reader's imagination. You need both writer's eyes and writer's ears—and a writer's heart.

Regardless, you don't ever want to forget your father's laugh.

PS If you were wondering, yes, my hair in that photo is made entirely of polystyrene, yet is completely edible.

4

Slipping Through Various Writing Fences

A few years ago, I had a peach of a ’68 Mustang. Though the creature drank gasoline like a Death Valley marathoner drinks water, it was a clean machine, and fun to drive. But like any car that’s 40+ years old, it had a loose tooth or two. So I scoured the InterWebz for Mustang parts suppliers, and bought a couple of items from Steeda, the company whose ad is pictured below.

Sidestepping the phallic push of this incomparable cold-air intake, I was struck by the flatly declarative copy of the ad. Not because it's sweepingly imaginative, but because there's such a narrow audience for whom it's intended. Cold-air intakes, that's what we got here—all other parties move on. Now the reason this struck me in particular is because on and off I mull whether my "one-size-writes-all" writing biz is too many things: flowers, trees, sky above, dirt below and cold-air intakes in between.

You see, besides fiction and essays, I write web copy, press releases, marketing collateral, ads, case studies, direct mail, and a bunch of tech content too. And I edit all of the aforementioned, and more. In fact, a while back I finished editing a small book on how to play any chord on the banjo. Though twangy, it was quite technical.

I think there's great value in seeing what kind of bedfellows writing for commercial reasons and writing for creative reasons are—the two types of writing aren't at some impassable divide. There's much to be gained in seeing how the approaches to both diverge and converge. And what's to be learned from the mixing. For me there is so much overlap, crisscross and inter-pollination (ooh!) between the two, because everything is built on the frame of compelling language, structure and the exploration of ideas.

Some fiction-only writers wrinkle their noses at the taint of the commercial writer, thought stained by a salesperson's strain to wiggle widgets at uninterested passersby. Some pedal-floored copywriters breezily dismiss the fevered character/plot/conflict workings of the fiction writer as the strivings of gossamer dreams, without chance for publication or pennies to follow.

I know otherwise. I write both; I know there is creative challenge, depth, value and fulfillment in both kinds of writing. Both commercial and creative writing can pull from deep sources, draw on emotional layers, and provoke rich thought. And dubbing one "creative" and one not isn't really accurate. Both can be creative. Or not.

Toward or Away from the Mountain?

I've always enjoyed the variety of writing/editing I do, but sometimes I fear there's a haphazard, slapdash aspect to the servings in my restaurant: can you trust a place to make great Chinese if they are advertising pizza too? And though I do OK with the dough, it's not like I can buy a wheelbarrow of Google stock.

Amusingly, in the way of when you begin to mull something, you'll see signposts and UFO sightings about that subject every-where, on a day when I was wrestling with my writing identity, I watched this commencement speech of Neil Gaiman's,[19] where Gaiman speaks about whether his ongoing work was taking him "toward or away from the mountain"—the mountain being his deepest goals. If away, he suggests to leave that work behind, if you can.

But "follow your bliss" doesn't precisely translate in this instance: I love the play of language even in a technical book on the banjo, but I don't feel passionate about that play. But then again, I'm further muddled about my mountain, because I waffle whether it's imperative to feel soaring passion about your work when it gives you pleasure at a basic level, and provides a sense of accomplishment, however ephemeral. I'm still mulling on passion's place, and where that place might be on my own map.

We all move through our days, trying to figure out what to do if we have a surgeon's hands and a troubadour's heart. (I have neither, but I do have impressively large feet.) In the meantime, I'll contact Steeda and see if they have made such a killing on cold-air intake sales that they can become my patron, and I can simply work on my new novel, which has suffered sore neglect lately.

To Niche or Not

Let's look further at the pigeonholing that can take place when writers are sorting out how to best make a living. Copywriters that have a clearly defined niche—"I write sales letters for mid-tier businesses selling nuclear-powered rabbits"—are both

---

[19] https://www.youtube.com/watch?v=plWexCID-kA

constrained by their choices and freed by them. They are constrained in that they may have always dreamed of writing sales letters for nuclear-powered goat companies, but instead they are known as the rabbit guy, and thus they don't want to dilute their focused offering, and potentially blur the boundaries of their defined space.

However, they are freed from casting their "I-need-new-work" lines in the thistle-tangled fields of businesses small, medium and large, who might peddle soap made from recycled comic books, or tongue scrapers for denture wearers. Generalist copywriters tend to a casual work garden of mingled (and sometimes flopping) stalks, colors and scents, while the specialist might have a sturdy monocrop of clients and cutoff dates.

From all I've confessed above, you might guess that I'm a generalist.

The 360-degree Rotating Exorcist Head

I've thought about trying to restrain my 360-degree rotating *Exorcist* head (minus green spewings) of writing endeavors, but it's just not my nature. While I can admire the ferocity of focus some copywriters employ, I can't join their ranks—I don't think I could breathe. And, genial bigot that I am, I have to sing the praises of the generalist's keys, because polymath writing pursuits are inherently interesting for their variety. A while back, I took a tally of the projects I worked on in one month, to wit:

- I finished an article for *Fine Books and Collections* magazine on the makers of exquisite and zany handmade books, touring the U.S. in their gypsy wagon.

- Finished editing a book on social media for nonprofits.
- Edited the first in a series of short books on *Nonverbal Communication in Dentistry.*
- Wrote logo taglines suggestions for a home design and remodel company, and begin writing their brochure copy.
- Discussed writing "replies" for a company that's developed an advanced virtual personal assistant chatbox app; the replies will cover the branching potentials for suggested questions that users might want answered.
- Discussed work with a company that needs someone to update the documentation for the new version of its novel-writing software.
- Wrote my two monthly articles (a recurring gig) for an Airstream publication's email newsletter.
- Sent out queries for a variety of articles, many of them travel-related (though a few were about whiskey and one about old cars).
- Sent out short older short stories of mine to some lit magazines.
- Berated myself for pausing in what had been a steady (and productive!) half-hour of writing per day on my novel, having used various holidays (even upcoming ones) and modest personal road-bumps for an excuse for not doing the work. Get after it, man!

Building Expertise, by the Paragraph and by the Project

Now, I have varying degrees of expertise in the areas above, but having written and edited nonfiction books, having written question-and-response dialog for software products, having written three novels and a book of short stories, having written and won awards for many travel pieces, having written brochures, heck, having written lots of grocery lists, I'm confident I can deliver what each organization needs, granting the many iterations of review and rewrite that some projects necessitate. For many writers like me, once you write website copy for a company, they may call you later to write headlines for an ad.

You might not have written headlines for ads before, but the good generalist will always pipe up with a merry "Yes!" when asked about their ability to write a heady headline. Many fundamental writing skills translate across boundaries—cross-writing is often more comfortable than cross-dressing. (High-heeled pumps just don't work well with my size 13s.) So, if you are breaking in to the copywriter's fold, and you're thinking that you could write sales letters not only for the nuked goats and rabbits, but perhaps for radium-isotope gerbils too—go for it. Next thing you know, you're a reptiles-with-battery packs specialist too.

Shaving the Cat and Other Specialist Pursuits

OK, pretending you'd asked in the first place, I want to wrap up the question of whether a business writer should be monogamous or be the genre-jumping playboy or playgirl. But first, let's discuss that cat-shaving: Foremost, you have to make sure that the nib of your fountain pen is VERY sharp—cats can be pretty critical of a sloppy shave. If you're not a pen-based cat shaver yourself, you absolutely must find a specialist—a mere penknife dog-shaver or needle-nose pliers hamster-hair plucker won't do, no matter if they have the skill basics.*

You'll find a lot of declarations online from successful creatives that having a niche is key. Every time I read one (and the arguments are sound) it has caused me to reflect that I not only shave cats, dogs and hamsters, but balloon animals too. My trouble is, as I've pirouetted around and about above, that I truly love the variety of writing a writer can do, and dabble in so many of its forms. And, well, there are bills to pay.

Ages back, I spent long years writing user manuals for software, and marketing pieces to flank the documentation. But as the Monty Python skit goes, "I don't want to own land; I want to *sing!*" (Translation: I want to write fiction. So I do that too.) One of the reasons my sweetheart angled to meet me, those many years ago, was because she wanted to meet someone who wrote the back-side descriptions for the photographs on pretty notecards. Guilty. And I find the personal essay to be a potent form for persuasion, polemic or poetic meandering, so it's a genre I return to again and again.

I've even been forced by a certain criminal musician/canny marketer/business maven/book-publishing madman, Joel D Canfield,[20] to write songs. Torment though it be, it was torment sweet. And then there's the YouTube indulgence—look mom, I can make videos too!

Peeling Twain's Onion by Way of Butterfly Wings

I think there is some danger in the dilution of dilettantism. But my hero, Mark Twain, wrote plays (badly), essays, poems, short

[20] http://joeldcanfield.com

stories, novels, advocacy pieces, travel articles, satire, straight journalism, handbills, speeches, jokes—and if you dip your toes into a wide reading pond, you'll be convinced that he must have sat down and decided to write an entire book of quotations. (Twain had a cat named Blatherskite, but he probably would have procured an outside vendor for the shaving.)

One of the intrigues about being an enthusiast about a subject or person is that once you start poking about, there seems to be a bottomless rabbit hole of information. And that hole can be well off the main road of what's normally shared among the broad population. Now I'm not talking about true obsession, where perhaps you know more about the Morpho butterfly than its mother did, where you skip lunch then dinner sitting on the floor of a bookstore a continent away from your home because you'd heard they had a dusty tome by the premiere 18-century entomologist who also skipped most meals in favor of studying the Morphos. Not that kind of obsession, my pretties.

No, I'm referring to something more than the mere fan, but less than the stalker. As an aside, there are the rare polyglots who are able to tiptoe close to obsession's stage while still staying out of its brightest footlights, and yet own another stage all their own. For example, going back to our fluttery friends, when Vladimir Nabokov wasn't writing one of his remarkably layered, seriocomic novels, he spent serious time researching butterflies, publishing many monographs that professional lepidopterists recognized as authoritative.

He once commented, "The pleasures and rewards of literary inspiration are nothing beside the rapture of discovering a new organ under the microscope or a never-documented species on a mountainside in Iran or Peru. It is not improbable that had there been no revolution in Russia, I would have devoted myself entirely to lepidopterology and never written any novels at all."

Looking at Layers Leads to More Layers

This is a hide-and-seek way of getting to my main topic: how people and things are multilayered, and once you start pulling at the onionskin of a topic or character, there's always another skin underneath. Case in point: I read a book a while ago titled, *Twain's Feast: Searching for America's Lost Foods in the Footsteps of Samuel Clemens.*[21] Now, were this work "... in the footsteps of Mamie Eisenhower," I probably—and no insult to Mamie—would have picked it up with mild amusement and then let it flit from memory forever.

But because it's Mark Twain, and I am more than a simple fan (though not obsessed, no, that's not the beating of my hideous heart!), I read it with great pleasure, for the author Andrew Beahrs combines his careful and light-hearted research into Twain's writings on American food with Beahrs's travels around the country trying to locate and eat that very food, which in the case of the prairie hens of Illinois proves ecologically difficult, and that of stomaching the ideal stewed raccoon a mite unpalatable.

---

[21] http://www.amazon.com/Twains-Feast-Searching-Americas-Footsteps/dp/B004HEXSN6/

From the Grubby to the Gracious

But it's the flavor of Twain's voice that comes through with spice, particularly when he lavishes angel-winged admiration on an American dish and contemptuous skewering on an insipid counterpart found elsewhere. His hilarious railings against spineless European coffee and expoundings on the glories of a stout cup of good American coffee do make one wonder what happened between Twain's time and our parents' days with the Folgers. Twain was uniquely suited to comment on the breadth of American food, for he palavered with the powerful in the boardrooms of the Eastern Seaboard, grubbed among the grubs in the grubbiest makeshift mining towns in dead-dry Nevada, and of course moved through the shoals and the high waters of foodstuffs up and down the mighty Mississippi, both in his boyhood and as a steamboat pilot.

I want to return to my original spiraling rabbit hole, for it's in the reading of the table tastes of a famous person that you consider how layered a life is, how layered all our lives are. Twain could be, in turn, a kitten-loving sentimentalist, a flinger of flaming arrows against the establishment, a provocateur who spoke truth to power, and yet one who cultivated the company of barons of industry. A man of spectacular fame, yet of multiple spectacular failures and deeply public sorrows. His onion had many skins, and reading this off-center book tells me there are skins I'll never know, on him and so many other subjects.

Yeah, Well, I Invented the Crossbow

Not that long ago I heard my girlfriend Alice tell one of my old friends on the phone that she had spent time a long while back to learn how to play the harmonica. Really! Who knew? Good instruction that, a reminder that thinking we know all that a person is about is a kind of blindness, because there are always layers unseen.

One thing though: Twain sang the praises of the 19-century oysters and mussels of the San Francisco Bay. That's going much too far—I vigorously object. Oysters and mussels: gut-tugging expressions of some bronchial character, a kind of simpering slime. Though on the subject of maple syrup, I share his every sentiment.

Getting back to shaving cats and shaving genres, I'll have to keep mulling over how I can trim my own whiskers. Some multi-niched writers (a chiropractor's dream) suggest to have separate websites for your separate specialties. I'm not sure I want my travel-writer self to be a website away from my marketing-writer self. I like them all to be on the same—crowded— page.

I know I've spent the last few pages talking mostly about the copywriting angle, but I will be discussing writing both fiction and non (and nonsense) in the Writing Structures section to come. Storytelling is a sacred art—even silly storytelling. And as I've tried to point out, both the fiction writer and the copywriter are weavers of tales.

**[Note to self: write synopsis of "Convincing Your Cat to Settle for Monthly Shaving" essay.]*

5

Writing Structures: Words, Sentences, Punctuation Marks—Oh My!

We've talked about opening your senses to the writing potentials in every glance, whisper or buttery taste of a croissant, on to the elements that have moved from your writer's mind onto the page. (Or are currently in motion.) This chapter is going to look at some writing structures, from words on their lonesome to words strung together. And even look at some of the string—the punctuation that pulls some phrases together and pushes others apart.

To begin: Writers can have a volatile relationship with words, often loving the little darlings when they line up in convivial co-operation. Sometimes words supply delight even when sentence forms are abused to torque a subject or vandalize a verb. "Words, yes, friends all!" the hoodwinked writer declares.

Until the words land on the page with an audible clunk, or when an apt phrase or exact expression can't be found no matter how deep the writer shovels into her soul. "Words, damn them, unreliable curs!"

I feel my own little death when I can't summon the rhythmic bits of language that brick out a character or spin a scene, no matter fiction or fact. But here, I want to talk about appreciating a certain sense of words as objects, a savoring of the spice from a word stew.

Feeling a Word's Curves

In this case, I'm not talking about meanings; I'm referring to loving the *feel* of a word, its texture, whether it's silky or scratchy, the odd combo of visual/visceral sensation you might get in your head from processing the very spelling of a word. You know, when looking a word gives you this kind of sensation:

Yes, I just gave you this car

That kind of word sensitivity started young in me too—maybe it was all those ice-cream brain freezes that cooled my cranium. [Note: your ideal situation may involve trapeze acts, Mars trips or dancing monkeys—indulge me in the Bentley. It is my name, after all.]

Anyway, I had an early awareness of the weight of words, and some I gravitated to some more so than others. For instance, words with "x" in them, like *bollix* or *flummoxed.* Do those give you the little frisson I'm alluding to? And how certain words feel just right in their denotation: *queasy* has that little lurch or drop in its letter construction—in its stomach—that is carried through in its definition. Or a word like *morbid:* it has a deliciously dark feel.

Lovers of words have close cousins—lovers of the very letters that comprise the words. And there's a couple of roads those letter lovers drive: one where they enjoy seeing certain letter arrangements, getting a visual delight from seeing a particular dance of letters. I get a kick out of seeing a word like "lagniappe," as much as I like "flummoxed," and "bollixed." Perhaps it's their alliterative alliances, the letter twins hopscotching, arms entwined. But it's not just a double consonant that charms—"chockablock," "whisper," "pendulum"—the list of eye-candy words for me is endless.

I've heard it said by some comedians that some words, by their letters alone, are funny. Words that start with "k" or the k sound, for instance. Probably why I like the sound of the word *crapulous*—or maybe it just harkens to my Coca Cola-crapulous days behind the gargantuan brandy snifter in which I housed and hogged down all that carbonated sugar water as a child.

Speaking of aural bites that are sweet: if you're like me, and as I mentioned earlier, you hear the words in your head as you read, particular letter combos ring a brighter bell in the mind's auditorium. I'm a slow reader anyway, but when I see a word that touches me both visually and aurally, I'll say it aloud a few times, mouthing its syllabic shape. Hey, there are no horses around to spook, so I'm safe. I even like words about language: *diphthong.* Yes!

Digging Through Your Dictionaries

I wrote an essay a long while back for a magazine called *Verbatim,* about the crazy collection of dictionaries I had, and how fun it is to just flip through them and look for words that have a furry feeling, or a sinister sparkle, or a wry rictus. It's a challenge to look through any dictionary page and *not* see some words that make you squint or grimace or grin.

Like your words 'lectronic? There are bunches of word sites, but here are a couple of fun ones: Wordnik[22] and Wordoid.[23] Wordnik has a nice interactive aspect where you can upload your own usage notes, comments and citations to their word examples. Wordoid lets you play with made-up words. But don't let your mother catch you.

---

[22] http://www.wordnik.com/

[23] http://www.wordoid.com/

Words: The Cat's Meow

Let's extend the word-delirium a bit: the Shelf Awareness[24] daily compendium of bookish (but never boorish) news revealed this statement from author Rick Riordan a while back about something he learned in his Egypt-themed novel research:

I did quite a bit of research, and had shelves of books on hieroglyphs and how magic pertained. The ancient Egyptians considered all writing magic. They had to be careful: if they created the word "cat," they had to deface it slightly, because they believed they could create a cat. The idea was that the ultimate form of magic was to speak and the world began. You see that influence in the Gospel of John: "In the beginning was the Word." All these ancient cultures dovetail, and they were all forming and evolving at the same time.

Behold the power of words! (Note: I spent all day writing variants of "Jaguar" yesterday, but no car appeared. I did see an old cat move haltingly through the yard, however...)

So, feel the curve of your words, know which ones excite and enchant, which are sturdy soldiers, and which weak-kneed wastrels. You'll never be able to truly tame them, but sometimes just getting them to play nice with one another is a mountain topped.

[24] http://www.shelf-awareness.com/

Working With Your Word Tree

Let's imagine you were hungry for some syllables, so you walked over to your yard's word tree. Word tree fruit always hangs in clusters of three, so you pick a triad with your left, and one with your right. You gobble the first cluster, discovering only after you chew that those three words were "rectal," "putrefy" and "termagant." Spitting the half-eaten leavings of those words onto the ground, you pop the other bunch in: they are "shimmer," "honey" and "moonlight." You chew with appreciation, because we taste words by their sounds, and the sounds of the first bunch were sour and those of the second sweet.

Of course, it's difficult to divorce the sounds of words from their meanings, and one man's *rectal* might be another's *moonlight.* But paying attention to how your writing sounds, how words taste in your head and in your customers' heads, can be key to delivering a tasty—and persuasive—message. And it's not simply that one clanging gong of a word in a sentence can make a reader wince—a sentence is composed of a sisterhood of words, and if one sister has a bad cold and can barely speak while another is so much taller than the others that her voice shoots over the others' heads, well, that's a sentence in a crisis relationship.

Consider these sentences:

- Mobile technological developments indicate concatenating aspirational undertakings by industry heads.
- Communication dreams are no longer schemes.

Either might serve as the introductory sentence for a white paper on new telephone technology. But the first makes for poor sonic footing: it clumps polysyllabic terms, the sound architecture of which causes one to climb up the tilted towers of its syllables and quickly topple. There's no space to gain a purchase, to scan for the landscape ahead. Hearing that sentence in your head is a series of lurches and stutters.

Don't Bump Your Nose on Your Sentences

The second, admittedly more abstract than the first, invites you to walk its rhythm without spraining an ankle. There is a beat and a measure to the sentence that is more balanced, more musical. Which sentence invites you to take the hand of the next, and which has you bumping your nose on a door that you didn't see? You need to check a sentence for its pulse: every sentence has tone, cadence, and pacing. If your sentences are written so some of the word sisters in the sorority carry those hand buzzers—when they clasp palms with the word next to them, there's an unsettling shock—your readers will draw back, rather than move forward in the reading.

The easiest way to do this is to read your writing aloud after it's written. Hear whether it flows or fumbles. Become conscious that a well-placed comma can invite a sentence to catch its breath, or that the exclusion of that comma can spark an agreeable acceleration. Even complex sentences, with potentially cumbersome clutches of words, can be structured so that they are a series of smooth steps, or if need be, a graduated set of invigorating leaps. The artful mixing of Anglo-Saxon bread with Latinate butter, short words and long, ones with internal rhyme that gather tightly with their cousins, a two-word sentence next to a twelve-worder—here you have a well-tuned orchestra of words, not a dissonant squawking.

Henry James famously said that *summer afternoon* are the two most beautiful words in the English language. That's arguable, of course, but Henry could feel—could hear—that a certain succession of letters, of syllables, of sounds are felt and heard in the mind as being pleasing or painful. (James himself perpetrated paragraphs of such intricately twining phrase and clause that you couldn't locate the originating verb with a microscope, but on this summer afternoon in question, he's clear.)

Consider that words have both aural shapes and textures that are felt and heard in the mind. Writing that sounds ugly is less persuasive. (Unless you playing with foul-faced words for effect, a different matter entirely.) So, pay attention to the sounds and the shapes of your words. Make them swim, spin or sigh in the auditorium of the imagination rather than crash or clatter. Your audience will rise to their feet to applaud, rather than to run.

How Word Seeds Make Word Trees

Talking about word trees does make me think of how you can use word seeds. When you begin a writing project, business or not, the blank page can look like a yawning abyss. You don't even want to approach the edge of that first line, because all that emptiness reminds you of how far you have to go to get to the other side. Despair sets in, the mind reels, the writing well goes dry. But there's a way any writing project can go from bud to blossom to bouquet: word seeds.

Word seeds are what I've used for years to blunt the fangs of any writing tiger, and make that kitty end up purring in my lap. Word seeds are in essence quick notes—and sometimes a single word—that vividly capture a concept. They are the pre-writing batter that makes the best cakes, because their ingredients are structural elements—ones that can grow to make the sum of their parts a sweet, risen whole.

Say you are supposed to write the elements of a complex landing page for a marketing campaign selling shoes for poodles. Do you try to write the whole cussed thing in one setting and watch it die a'borning? Do you even want to risk trying to get the headline and first paragraph down in one run, fail, and rail against the cosmos? No, you use word seeds.

You scribble something like:

- *Curly toes to match curly fur?*
- *Tie them with teeth*
- *Velcro*
- *Matching capes*
- *Athletic and evening wear*

The Oyster, Sand, Pearl Effect

And so on. Word seeds supply you several benefits: listing terms and phrases in pre-composition sticks them like a swizzle stick into the soft folds of your mind. Believe it or not, they have that oyster/sand/pearl effect. Even if you might not feel them, they are scritching and scratching in those soft folds and changing from seed to sprout. Going back to them after a day or two has always proven fruitful for me. Review the seeds, and then sentences or entire paragraphs will appear fully formed, the whole cloth made of the thin threads of your notes.

Another benefit is that writing down quick notes provides the security that you are moving forward in the project (and indeed by such notes you are, simple as they can be). Plus, reading them provides a prompt that spurs new seedings. You can later organize them in a raw order of how the piece of writing might unfold, and that act too almost always spills new seeds from your fervid brain.

So:

- Don't discount the value of even a single word being a springboard to writing an ad, an essay, a marketing campaign for poodle shoes, a scene in a story
- Use the right, descriptive, vibrant words, not vague ones
- Carry a notepad with you for when you're away from your computer
- Re: above, write legibly. (For me, this is impossible, but perhaps your handwriting isn't the result of alien probing)
- Use word seeds to break down a writing project into manageable increments

I finished a novel by writing only a half-hour a day over a period of months. I seeded the end of one day's writing with a few words that are scene prompts—they caffeinated the next day's work. This very section is self-referential: it sprung from a few phrases I'd dashed off days earlier.

Thus, use word seeds: scrawl them on a napkin, scribble them on your palm, write them in melted chocolate. Verily, they will grow.

How Basketball Is Like Sentence Building

It's easy to tire of the exhausted sports metaphor: "He dropped the ball; it's in your court; that was a slam dunk; we had to punt." Most clichés have altogether lost their pepper, but ones involving sporting feats—employed with particularly ruthless disregard for their actual applicability in the business world—seem to have withered before they even rounded second base. So for me to drag you, punting and dunking, into an arena where basketball is used as a metaphorical muse for writing might cause you to think this is an exercise in sweaty nonsense.

And yet. A while back, I went to a professional basketball game in Santa Cruz, where the NBA's Oakland Warriors have their D (developmental) League team. If you've watched (or even played) much basketball, it can look like a manic maelstrom of movement, the ball whipping from player to player, defenders darting, many a feint and many a collision of shoulders and legs. And that's just on one possession of the ball. It begins all over again when the ball changes hands.

But when a team is running the court in high gear, when passes are crisp, cuts away from or to the basket are sharp, when a jump shot floats off the fingers of the shooter like a soft fluttering dove to nestle in the net, it's a thing of beauty. That's how it is when words, sentences, paragraphs are working right. There is motion in language, there is exchange of motion, there is anticipation and delivery. The smooth pause can lead to an explosive conclusion; a quiet turn of phrase can open up a delicate cat-and-mouse communication, one that can lead to a ferocious end or a finessed bit of finery.

Words Work in Teams

While I watched the action on the court, word weirdo that I am, I thought how words work in teams, how there is an energy exchange between words, and how when you move them around in different ways, their meaning is recast. So it is with the movement on the court. Of course, the court movement can have a slapdash, arrhythmic outcome, as can a poorly rendered sentence or paragraph. Use the wrong verb and your sentence sags. For most teams, put your center out on top of your offense in place of your point guard, and watch your offense go to sleep.

I also started thinking of how your first-string team (your conflicted protagonist, the opening lines of your blog post, the value prop of your business) is supported by the structural material of your second-string team (the backstory, the summary section of the blog, the features/benefits box), and how your bench material can hold the dam's undercarriage together while the prime design shines. But then I realized I was mixing sports metaphors with other writing clichés, kind of like making a meal of old boxing gloves and thumbtacks, and nobody's hungry for that.

Slam dunk!

Take a Punctuation Mark Out to Lunch

OK, so we've been wrangling with words—let's bring the dissection tools a bit closer and look at those traffic cops of words: punctuation marks. And what better way to talk about anything than to begin with a joke?

A comma, a period and a semicolon walk into a bar ... oh, wait! I can't finish the joke; I forget how it's punctuated. (Wow, tough crowd.) But punctuation's no joke, my friends—each punctuation mark has a grave (or acute) purpose: sometimes bearing a serious slant, sometimes swinging a strong, straight shoulder to torque the weight of words through thought rivers. Think of the cymbal crash of the exclamation point, the yearning intrigue of the question mark, the potential hidden menace of the semicolon.

But behind the sober, workaday faces of those little bits of pause and check, it's not so black and white. Every punctuation mark has its own personality, much more idiosyncratic than that of a bland worker wielding the traffic signals of sentence flow. Like any of us, they appreciate the anonymity of a job well done, but at the same time, they don't mind letting on that there's a purple sash under the white cotton shirt.

No Comedy, the Comma

Consider the comma. If the period is a full stop, the comma is an intake of breath, the holding of the conductor's baton before the wrist is flicked and the words swirl. The comma is the odalisque of marks; concepts nestle within its coy curves. And as with curves, one pauses at entry and accelerates away. The comma, a curved finger that both beckons and halts.

Whereas the semicolon, top hat and all, is truly the formal gentleman of punctuation. But look closely; the semicolon also has a rakish element, the Frenchman with a beret, who with no small show of bonhomie will ask you to stop for a moment, have a smoke, a bite of croissant, invite you to consider the revolution. Then and only then can you march on. The semicolon, mannered, foppish, sincere.

The colon is much more the fussy passport clerk: stop, stop, papers please, now! You can see the words piling up, bumping behind the knees of the words ahead, but there's no getting around the colon; words must heel. The colon, officious, waxed, but willing to negotiate—as long as standards are obeyed.

But the colon never yells. No such constraints hold the exclamation point, the train crossing of marks, all flashing lights and clanging bells. We dread the shout of *exclamation point!* in a crowded theater. More dreadful yet, its dull employ as the marketer's cudgel. Usage is a matter of taste, and the exclamation point is the habanero.

There's something visibly friendly about the apostrophe, particularly when it's engaged to signal the omitted letter. The ensuing contraction doesn't bespeak a sense of loss, but rather is casual and merry, there's a genial wave. Heaps o' fun. Down the 'atch. All's right with the world. The apostrophe is utterly offhand, but trustworthy.

I Stop for Periods

Then there's the swallowtail coat of the full stop, the period. The world threatens to end with not a whimper, but a period. It's a sententious mark, full of itself, a round of circular reasoning. It's remarkable that something so even, so un-elliptical (unless you add a couple of kissing cousins) has such an ego, but there it is. Period.

The parenthesis is sturdy, but a bit dull. (All punctuation marks are punctual, except for the closing parenthesis, which because of the curve of its leg, always arrives at the end of the sentence.) We'll skip past its breathy embrace.

Don't forget that National Punctuation Day is coming—be sure to take a semicolon out to lunch.

Skipping Through the Sentence Pudding

Punctuation: it's so much fun, why stop with taking your favorite marks out to lunch? Why not take the little devils out for some dainty skipping through some sentence pudding? Let's skip:

It was brought to my attention (I love the phrase, because I envision velvet-liveried footmen bringing a notion—one resting on a purple pillow—to me) that there is a book that takes a studied look at the history of parentheses, their use over the ages, their value as a species, their contributions not only to the literature, but as an aesthetic component of thought.

It is called *But I Digress.*[25] Not only is this a work of 344 pages, its purchase price is $195 last time I looked. My.

Because I enjoy the employment (though not the moral obligations) of a good pair of parentheses myself, that spurred me to consider how the lovely little tocks and notches of punctuation create a soft side-current in the river of thought, an accent note, like how you might detect a whiff of elderberries in your Cabernet Franc, though its main train to your nostrils is peopled with toffee and raisin bread. Punctuation is the conductor's wand to the orchestra's melding of swelling verbal notes. (Oh yeah, you can quote me on that.)

That got me to mulling over how the use of punctuation in some spare composition—an epitaph, say—might be the axis for delivering meaning. On the subject of epitaphs, writers should always write their own. You could do worse than emulate the sing-song declarativeness of some of the lines in the famed Monty Python "Dead Parrot" sketch:

- He's pining for a fjord
- His metabolic processes are now history
- He's run down the curtain and joined the bleeding choir invisible
- THIS IS AN EX-PARROT!

---

[25] http://www.amazon.com/But-Digress-Exploitation-Parentheses-English/dp/0198112475/

Categorizing Your Tombstone Tokens

Fine epitaphs, but in regards punctuation, those Pythonesque parrotings are lacking. Consider a few categories:

Friendly – A simple phrase like "Loads o' fun" works well. The apostrophe indicating the omitted "f" is casual and merry, and bespeaks geniality. What about an Elizabethan elision: *O'er teacakes and waistcoats, I did preside.*

Marketing – Employ the marketer's cudgel: the exclamation point. Something like *Dead! Thoroughly! Special Offer to Repeat Visitors!*

Brevity – Though he spoke it, the one-word sign-off for Dan Rather's news broadcast all but shouted (and because it was one word, also intimately whispered) that the word ended with a full stop: *Courage.* You could try something like *Stewing.* Or maybe *Ennui.*

Needs Answering – And the interrogative ending will surely get your plot's visitors mulling over meaning: *Mind getting me some water?* Or, *Do you know that hat makes you look like a monkey?*

Pauses and Ponderings – I like a nice mix of colons and semicolons on a stone: *Note to self: I'll nap here; at some point, I'll have to do laundry.*

Corral Your Word Cattle – And of course we have to visit what prompted this business in the first place, the exalted parenthesis: *Keep the peace (and keep your hands off my wife).* Or, *Here I lie. (Hey, it's better than stealing.)*

Closing with a Bang

You may be thinking I'm belaboring these poor barely nourished marks, and I earlier addressed that charming coy curve, the comma, above; we'll have to review the happy hand-me-the-baton linker, the hyphen and that dashing fellow—the dash—another time. But I do want to close with a bang: an interrobang,[26] that is.

A combination of the question mark and the exclamation point (dubbed on Wikipedia as a "quesclamation" mark), the bang is implying the asking of a question in a heightened state. Perhaps for an epitaph, something like *Christ, all this and they give me a view of the Safeway* [The funny (?) thing here is that the formatting software I'm using won't display the interrobang at the end of the Safeway sentence. So I'll use this: #$@!!%#!]

Grammar: It's Funnier Than it Tastes

Gadzooks, I was able to slip my little dithering about punctuation right by you, like a Bob Feller (way back, in geezer baseball times) fastball. Maybe you're even willing to peek at some postulations about grammar.

Most people equate discussing grammar with chugging molten lava, but I know you're bigger than that, so let's grammarize.

My parents offered me a sip of a martini when I was seven or eight years old. I recall recoiling in disgust from its sharp, medicinal tang: "How can you drink that? It's terrible!" Yet a crisp, cold martini on a Friday at five now seems the ideal reward for a week's labor.

---

[26] http://en.wikipedia.org/wiki/Interrobang

It is always amusing to remember the heated declarations you make in earlier days—"When I get outta this house I'm never going to cut my hair, ever!"—and to consider the cooling of those declarations when they're set out for a stretch on time's countertop. That's why I had to laugh when I saw the grammatical term "Future in the Past" in a grammar book the other day. Let's relate it to the martini: who wants to read a grammar book for pleasure? Think of squirming away from grammar lessons in grade school; it would have been a difficult decision to determine whether you'd rather have a root canal or listen to someone prattle on about grammar.

But I've been in the writing trade for a while, and I think it's good (and even fun) to continue to sharpen your tools. One of the grammar books I read was *Grammatically Correct: The Essential Guide To Spelling, Style, Usage, Grammar and Punctuation.*[27] Yes, you're right, I'm a riot at parties.

Anyway, in one of the sections on tenses (stay with me, people), there's a discussion of some tense variants that are little used, and the one that seemed delightful to me was "future in the past," described as expressing the idea that at an earlier time point, there had been an expectation that something would later happen.

Dig that! So, if you say, "I had a feeling that you were going to bloat like a dirigible if you ate that entire cheesecake," you are using the future in the past tense. I also liked the further explanation that it doesn't matter if your future/pasting was

[27] http://www.amazon.com/Grammatically-Correct-Essential-Spelling-Punctuation/dp/1582976163

correct or not. So, we can all shoot to be soothsayers, but if that doesn't work out, we can go into accounting.

Yeah, I guess you had to be there. But just to push it further: over time, with different editions of yourself, you learn a bit more of who you are. That kid who spat out that martini would never have dreamed that something in a grammar book would delight him years later. He might have said, "I knew that Tom was going to hate martinis and grammar when he grew up." And he would have been wrong, but he would have crafted a fine future-in-the-past utterance. You live, you learn.

Stylish (and Amusing) Style Books

The worthy tome I recently finished—I told you I know how to have a good time—is Steven Pinker's *The Sense of Style*,[28] where that fellow with the rumpled hair "... applies insights from the sciences of language and mind to the challenge of crafting clear, coherent, and stylish prose." But there are so many style/grammar guides that are helpful, and even amusing, often for their outlandish example sentences. I've read a bunch of them and recommend many (don't want too many endnotes here, so Google 'em):

Eats, Shoots and Leaves
Woe Is I
The Transitive Vampire (or others in Karen Gordon's series)
Spunk and Bite
Sin and Syntax

[28] https://www.amazon.com/dp/B00INIYG74/

Stealing liberally from my forbears (though writing my own weird example sentences), I even wrote one[29] a few years back. No Strunk and White (or even Spunk and Bite), but fun.

And continuing to learn: that's a crisp, cold martini to me. I'll take two.

Short Pieces Have Plenty of Reasons to Live

So far in this structure section, we've been dealing with nails, bolts and brackets of composition: things like punctuation and words. Keeping up the carpentry metaphor, why not move into the posts and piers of writing: short pieces, mostly the kind that appear in magazines. Short stories are another discussion altogether.

[Note to quibblers: I am not exactly the handy type, though I can wield a paper towel with the best of them. So if hit my thumb with a mangled-metaphor hammer when I rhapsodize about the construction trades above, indulge me. I will reward you by not sending you any of my free verse.]

I had a tiny piece about the Las Vegas Hangover Heaven bus[30] published in *Draft* magazine. *Draft* is the highest-circulating craft-beer magazine, with a frothy lineup of stories about breweries, industry personalities and innovations in the brewing world. My little article is just a whisper of words, but I'm still happy to have it published, for a number of writing reasons.

---

[29] http://www.tombentley.com/guides/write_word_style_guide.pdf

[30] http://www.tombentley.com/HangoverHeaven.pdf

Many magazines today, from *Smithsonian* to *Seventeen*, have lots of small articles and light pieces in their brightly designed front (and sometimes back) pages. It speaks to the reading tastes of the Internet age: colorful and chunky. For writers, and especially ones trying to break in to a magazine, these areas (called "front of book" or FOB) can be a quick keyboarding to good money and wider opportunities.

Many magazine editors don't have the time or patience to try out an unknown writer on a feature piece, but query them on a 200- or 300-word filler article, and they will more often acquiesce. And those appetizer articles are often a way to set the table for a full-meal article later.

In the case of *Draft*, I'd written a long feature piece on moonshining for them a while back, so I know the editor. I pitched the Hangover Heaven piece as a feature, but was still happy when the editor came back with the offer to make it a short FOB article. Happy because those articles often pay .50 to $1 a word (the case here), and more so because it kept me fresh in the mind of the editor. I'm about to query her with another feature pitch this week because I'm fresh in the magazine and fresh in her mind.

Short Articles Can Pay the Long Green

Short is also sweet in terms of demonstrating that you can consistently carry a certain kind of article to completion. I just wrote my 12th FOB piece for *The American Scholar*, for a section called Works in Progress. These articles have all been 250-word pieces, which again pay well, word-wise. Better, after having written a few of these, the editor now inquires if I have any ideas for the next quarterly issue. I'm in good stead with that editor for stories to come—possibly longer stories to come—and potentially with editors of other good magazines, because the *Scholar* is a national magazine of high caliber, focusing on public affairs, literature, culture and more.

One other consideration on short pieces: you can often use the research done for a longer piece as the basis for another short article. I wrote an article for *Airstream Life* magazine on Edward Tufte, the professor who is famous for his work in rendering complex information into a comprehensible whole. He also is a designer of very fanciful sculptures, among them one that uses an Airstream in a most improbable way.[31] After I wrote the *Airstream Life* piece, I realized that some unused info and quotes from the interview could be shaped into a short piece for *The American Scholar.* Bingo, a twofer! (And I'm grateful that the editor of *Airstream Life* now brings potential stories to my attention as well, since I've written for him for years.)

So, don't think writing small pieces for magazines diminishes their stature. If they are big enough for a byline, they are big enough to stand on their own. And they can lead to bigger things down the road.

Bigger Ain't Necessarily Better

Besides, being short, you'll never have to worry about seeing all of that guck that's on the top of your refrigerator. Me being the long, lanky type, so shamed am I when I spot that accretion of

[31] http://www.edwardtufte.com/bboard/q-and-a-fetch-msg?msg_id=0003uU

grime that I have to stop the speechwriting I do for the American Graham Cracker Collection Society, and clean it immediately. But if you haven't been clued in, I'm still referring to *length*, not height, where bigger isn't necessarily better—in writing.

Another "short is the solution" situation comes to mind: I went to a Writer's Digest West writing conference in LA a couple of years back, and there I engaged in a frolicsome thing called a "pitch slam." A pitch slam isn't where you test your curveball to see if you can strike out Mike Trout; it's where a hoard of peevish, underfed literary agents listen to your strangled proposal for your book, and then press a button that puts you in a trash compactor, while you hear the waning sounds of their maniacal laughter.

The slam part is this: you have 90 seconds to pitch your book. Ninety seconds: that's easily enough time for me sit in front of the agent, swallow my tongue, fall to the floor and writhe spasmodically. When I scanned the agents that were available for this particularly torture, I saw that I had at least five chances to pitch—a fit—in front of them.

However, the event must have been organized by a lunatic prairie dog, who had no concept that putting 125 anxious writers in a shoebox-size room with horrible acoustics and snaking, tangled lines wasn't ideal. I ended up only being able to pitch two agents in the allotted time, one of whom requested (and then gently rejected) my manuscript. The fact that the Manhattans at the bar cost $17 each didn't prevent me from ordering two. But writing a pitch is still a good exercise, no matter how poorly mine went over.

Brevity Is the Soul of Lingerie

Writing short can be refreshing, like ice in your underwear. Writing short can also get practical results. I won a great MediaBistro Literary Festival online conference pass just by tweeting what I judged to be the best sentence I'd ever written. (Never mind, with counting the hashtag, that my first three choices were longer than Twitter's character count allows).

As Dorothy Parker said, "Brevity is the soul of lingerie." Thus, to display my lingerie, I entered a contest of the Gotham Writer's Workshop, requesting a 50-word monologue on suburban life in the 60s. Just for being one of the five finalists, I won two tickets to the Broadway revival of *Who's Afraid of Virginia Woolf.* Here's my entry, titled, *My Life, My Lawn.*

> *It's much more than the lawn. Sure, sure, a green, nicely trimmed lawn says something about attention, about reliability, about caring, dammit. But bigger: it's about soul. The clipped edge, the squared surface, the green greener than life itself: soul. Just a lawn? Like saying Lincoln was just a lawyer.*

It is fun to figure out how to squeeze a multi-points-of-view tragicomic opus into 90 seconds, without including all the sighs, cries and lies. (And hey, if any of you agents happen to read this, I don't *really* think you are peevish or underfed. I will remember all your children's birthdays forever.)

Banging the Bongo Drums of Brevity

You may be tiring of me banging on about the bongo drums of brevity (and using my own works as examples), but I hope they are illustrative of the value of binding up your words in a tight little box. See what a cruel but clever word master you can be?

A while back, I futzed away on a tiny short story for the *Esquire* Short-Short Fiction contest, which honored the magazine's 78th birthday by staging a contest for stories of 78 words. Mandated word counts are an interesting exercise: they are both constraining and liberating. Constraining, because if you go 79 words here, you're out. Also because they force you to examine every branch of your story's tree, and to see that a careful pruning can open up the air and the light in a tale (as well as a tree).

Word cages are liberating because knowing a story's boundaries allows you to map it all the more clearly. You chop that subordinate clause there because it droops too heavily with verbiage. You might even have to chop out a subordinate character for the very same reason. (Note: you cannot do this with your relatives.)

Shaping Stories by Word-Slicing

Thus, being told by a child "Tell me a story" can be so much more challenging than "tell me a story with a princess who bets on the horses and ends up becoming a big-wave rider in Hawaii." Riding the waves is easier when you can see their definition.

Also, there is an almost surgical sense of control when it's evident that you can change a sentence's flavor just by excising some sagging skin. Even the whisking away of a "that" or an "a" can put more pepper in a phrase.

Which reminds me of the Twain quote: "Substitute 'damn' every time you're inclined to write 'very'; your editor will delete it and the writing will be just as it should be."

War AND Peace? Please Choose

Sometimes writing to a theme and a word count is just plain fun. I had a piece come out in *Writer's Digest,* for their "Reject a Hit" page. The challenge is to act as though you were the cruel, benighted editor that turned away a literary classic, and you must do such in 300 words. As with that handicapping, wave-sailing princess, the theme constrains and liberates. Here's mine:

Mr. Tolstoy: Re: your "War and Peace" query—my God man, one word: editing! Readers today are busy counting the serfs, polishing their mazurkas and dusting their Pushkin collections. They haven't the stomach to digest a twelve-room dacha of a work. Think a brightly lit (but slight) tea garden of literature for today's busy readers, or at most an airy drawing room. And let's be reasonable—War AND Peace? Confine it to one, and save 350 pages.

Now, some specifics: Instead of the original Petersburg setting, it's best to confine the whole thing in a tiny village, eschewing all those dreary travel scenes. If I had to read again about the boorish behaviors of a panoply of grubby roadside characters, I'll scream! Keeping it to a village makes it more like a tidy play. In fact, perhaps this WOULD make a fine play—study your Chekov for pointers.

And let's avoid all that violence and mayhem; we can't found literary works on sensationalism, you know. And any drinking scenes have to go—that's a fusty Russian stereotype that could use refreshing. Perhaps all the villains could be low-level clerks? Everyone hates a clerk.

You do show some promise with character, though must you go on so? No more interminable sighs for the women, or long-winded hortatory oaths from the men; think clean, declarative, adjective-free sentences. It should go without saying that no women should die in childbirth, ugh! And really—including the French, even if the portrait is unflattering, in a popular novel? No. No French.

In summary, the work shows no small promise—but it's TOO LARGE! Tighten its belt, shave its unshorn soldiers, pare 10 peasants for every one saved, remove all those fluffy word-curtains and showy emotive splashes and you might have something here. In fact, this might make a perfect piece of flash-fiction. Cut it down to 500 words and re-submit.

And if you really want to put some tight wraps on your writing, hie on over to Smith Magazine,[32] home of the Six-Word Memoir project. Every day lots of folks work on putting their words on a diet by posting six-word stories. (Dirty trick: use hyphenated compounds and cheat!) The editors even collect some of the entry categories for publication in books. So get cracking, but remember: six words is a story, seven is a stultifying bore.

Writing Turkeys Still Have Some Trot

Let's move from writing short to writing with a tail. Turkey tails, that is. I want to talk about putting flavor in your writing, but again, like with writing short, you don't want to over-spice it. And again, I turn to my neighborhood's animal life to animate my angle.

---

[32] http://www.smithmag.net/

For the best part of last year and into this, around 20 wild turkeys have been strolling their gobbling paths through the open fields of my neighborhood. It's amazing when they cruise by the field close to my Airstream office, because they are startlingly big birds, and in their turkeyness, quite odd-looking ones too.

The turkeys visited in the early spring, and what better incentive for male turkeys to display their boorish ways? Then, the male birds would whip up their tail-feather tuxedo, to give the ladies a peek at the splendid side. If you don't spend a lot of time looking at a turkey's backside, you might never have seen their flashdance, where they fan those tail feathers in a broad semicircle, displaying the bright bands of color at feather's end.

It's an eye-catching sight, and an impressive one too. One of the reasons it impresses is that the birds don't do it constantly, so that the amazement threshold dims; instead, they putter and poke around, grubbing in the fields in their civilian clothes. It's only when some kind of unseen "Showtime!" signal occurs that they feel the need to fan out their deck of face cards, and then quickly put them away.

Just a Flash, and No More

The flash of color, of intrigue, of insight—I think that's what we should do with our writing. No one likes heavy writing, that draws attention to itself by pounding you in the face, then in the gut, then the face again. But what if, in what you're reading, a curtain quickly opens and you see something intriguing, only to have it close again? Wouldn't you read a bit further to see what's behind the curtain?

Though there are many ways to insert elements in your writing that might be considered revelations—surprise, your lead character was actually a love-struck alien from the 25th century!—here I'm just talking about interesting turns of phrase, vivid language used with sparing care. Flashes in writing are momentary: they offer a promise, provoke intrigue, suggest something more. It harkens to the same psychological mechanism of the slot machines: there are small payoffs (and they are loud and colorful) in between stretches of quiet. It's a mechanism you can use to send a flare of interest, no matter if you are writing business copy or a novel.

Words Take Wing

I'm a word guy first, so I gravitate toward language to put the trot in my turkeys. Be conscious of flat turns of phrase in your work, whether you type for business or for tale. Give flat phrases a face by filling in their features: stronger verbs, interesting syntax, varying sentence rhythms. Let's look at a standard sentence turkey, followed by one flashing his charms:

He walked unsteadily through the crowd.

He careened, he lurched, he staggered, he chugged—we see his tripping traipsings with more vigor, more clarity, more delight.

Rearranging how your words fall can make them rise:

Dullard: *Benjie was besotted, and his head lolled on his sloped shoulders.*

Benjie, Better: *Shoulders sloped, head lolling, see besotted Benjie.*

Even being conscious of the *sound* of words (and how they sound strung together) can give your writing resonance:

Barely a Sound: *He drove the taxi for hours through the dark streets of the suburban neighborhood.*

More Music: *He drove, the taxi's sharp lights sniffing out the darkened curbs, the dull patches of suburban lawn grey-green in the bleak light.*

Don't Troll the Thesaurus

I'm not suggesting here that you become a thesaurus troll, someone picking canned words from a list—thoughtless thesaurus use will only make your words listless. Many are the sentences that are best served with solid Anglo-Saxon words. I'm also not talking about using unusual words just for the sake of novelty. Look not to pad your sentences, but to spice them, with language that is your own—but perhaps your own language after additional caffeine. This kind of word-by-word, sentence-by-sentence vigilance might seem wearying, but more wearying is reading writing that has no spark.

Putting Some Mustard on the Turkey (and Adding Corn)

If you've every watched a turkey fly, you know it can look like someone tossed a large, unbalanced sack of feathers into the air. They are ungainly, awkward flyers, but they get the job done. And as I mentioned above, with their neck-stretching pecking-and-lunging walk, they can look peculiar on the ground too. But with that feather flash, they perform a magic trick: they turn their turkey trot into a show of style.

Yeah, I know—who wants to be identified as a turkey? But learning how to successfully write like a turkey has its benefits. As the old saying goes (with some editing), every turkey has its day. Show your tail feathers.

I am only too delighted to move from talking about adding turkeys to your writing to adding corn. Soon I should have an entire barnyard of clucking characters here with which to populate your writing.

Dizzy with Disney

When I saw some time back that the antique Disney film *Swiss Family Robinson*[33] was on the old movie channel I favor, I had to take a peek—after all, at 6 years old, I'd thrilled to its elemental (and elementary) charms at its theatrical release, more than 50 years ago. Thinking I'd only watch for a few minutes, I wanted to see if any of its hoary elements might still provoke a gasp—or, more likely, an unintended laugh.

Indeed, though the film is filled with Disney cheese, I gobbled the whole damn thing up, watching entranced from one cornball scene to the next. It struck me that a good story is a good story, even adorned with some fairy-tale frippery. In a nutshell, Swiss Family Robinson is the tale of a family shipwrecked on a small

[33] http://www.imdb.com/title/tt0054357/

island, having to make a life for themselves amidst deprivation, harsh elements and direct threats.

You just have to go with the fanciful unfolding that the family (still-vibrant parents and three boys of variable ages and temperaments) is able to build a multi-level home in the jungle that would put many avant-garde designers to shame, and are able to fend off a band of murderous pirates with bombs made of coconuts, gravity-tripped logs and pit-trapped tigers—oh my!

Take Characters. Put in Situations. Add Emotions. Stir.

But the tale has what it takes. There is:

Danger and Loss – Their boat and their dreams to move to a new country are dashed in a violent shipwreck scene, which they survive, only to wash up on an island populated with all kind of menacing beasts.

Discovery and Development – They work as a team to build their house, learn to scavenge for food, and explore the wilderness.

Desire and Romance – A pirate captive is freed, and he turns out to be a she, longed-for by both the oldest and middle boys, who get into a jealous (and amusing) rivalry.

Threat and Triumph – They are attacked by the pirates, and improbably vanquish them. Rescuers come, and mom and dad and most of the family decide to stay, because the life they've created is too good to leave.

All of this is mightily sprinkled with sentiment of the cloyingly Disneyish kind: a frightening depth of blondness in all the characters (well, they are Swiss), syrupy innocence, and some absolute absurdities: the island has pretty much every beast known to man on it, from tigers to elephants to ostriches to monkeys.

Even Cynical Bentley Filmgoers Still Crave a Good Story

But yet, a 50-year-old movie still worked in my snide head, because the storytelling was still vivid, and it employed those paragons of story architecture: colorful (albeit one-dimensional) characters, conflict and partial resolution, then add in colorful subplotting, and tension, all building to a satisfying, if sappy, denouement. Writers, take notes (and pass the popcorn).

Writing Funny

Now that I've added turkey and corn to your writing, I can't sidestep the inevitable: talking about writing and humor. Remember that old judge's old adage about porn, "I know it when I see it"? Humor is a bit like that: hard to pin down, but something that definitely prompts a reaction. Trying to enliven a piece of writing with humor can often let the air out of laughter's tires, but when you hit your punch lines, your audience often comes back for more.

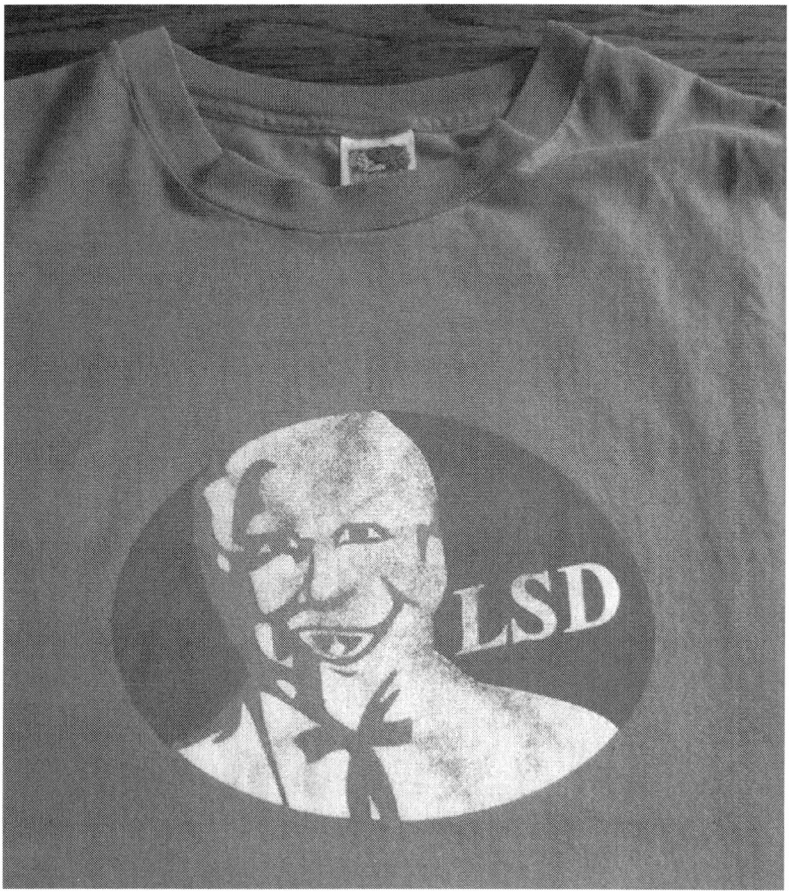

The image here is a photo of one of my favorite shirts. If it's not clear to you, it's Colonel Sanders with a maniacal look, with the unsubtle graphical suggestion that the good Colonel has had a snootful of LSD. That amuses me on several levels, but the one that's instructive here is based on a two-step of moving from familiar to farcical.

You can employ this comedic trip of incongruity in your writing (though never in your cooking).

Of course, the expression and interpretation of humor is as subjective as declaring that the piccolo is king of wind instruments, hands-down. (Never forget the panpipe!) What some folks think is funny is just whistling wind to others: Some jokes might have your entire Mongol horde spitting out their teeth, while another of the same caliber might only make your cat laugh. For some it's poop jokes, for some it's palindromes, and never the twain shall meet. (Except for this instance, since "poop" is a palindrome.)

So, neatly sidestepping the sheer subjectivity (and the poop) of our subject, I'll concentrate on a single comedic element that works for me as a writer, and as a consumer of comedy: incongruity. It's as broad as the princess with the corn stuck in her teeth, or as peculiar as a man in a business suit with briefcase walking a crocodile, or as off-balance as a garden gnome giving a speech on metaphysics to an assemblage of frogs.

The Setup

Dave Barry is a master of the incongruous in his writing, and a lot of the funny in what he does is structured on a one-two-three of situations or circumstances, where the one and the two are prosaic, but the three is preposterous—but the preposterousness only works because the one and the two are banal enough to lull the reader, and the three puts a moustache on the coffee cup. What's THAT doing there?

Here's a Barry quote from an interview that asked him what book changed his life. (Note, Barry has said or written much funnier stuff than this, but this is a good example of the structure of what I'm talking about).

Barry's reply: "*The Brothers Karamazov,* by Dostoevsky. I was supposed to read it my freshman year in college, but it's 18 million pages long and I could never get past the first 43. Nevertheless I wrote a paper about it, and I got an OK grade, which taught me that I could write convincingly about things I did not remotely understand. This paved the way for my career in journalism."

Emily Dickinson, Notable Joker

It's the old bada-bing, done twice here by Dave. Straight answer, a bit of elaboration, and then a kicker; rinse and repeat. The incongruity I'm talking about is often a matter of rhythm: you set up the reader by offering some conventional understanding, and then you goose that understanding with a cheeky thrust. Though it's not always going for the belly laugh; sometimes it's more a "Huh? Ah, you're nuts." But nuts in a winning way. It's a variant of ol' Emily Dickinson's "Tell all the truth but tell it slant."

So exactly HOW do you do this? Sheesh, I'm no Svengali; when you try to write funny, it often comes out a miserable hairball-like thing, shaggy and sad. It's more of an attitude or perspective. Check out this article[34] I wrote for the LA Times on the travails of travel a bit back; it has some of what I mean. Sometimes it's as "simple" as that Jack Benny stare and shrug that coming from another man would only produce indifference, but from Benny it was hysterical. And sometimes you have to go out on a limb: you have to give an avuncular icon dangerous drugs. It's the Colonel that gets fried, not that chicken of his.

---

[34] http://www.tombentley.com/spidertales.pdf

Bonus Colonel Sanders Sighting!

One reason why I probably find the Colonel reeling on chemicals comic is that when I was 11 or 12, I was selling candy bars outside the local liquor store (it had lots of traffic) in my hometown, fundraising for my Catholic grammar school. I was with my best friend, who can verify: we sold a candy bar to Colonel Sanders. I'm not talking about a guy dressed up like Colonel Sanders: this WAS the Colonel, with the white suit and string tie, the man himself. He was alone, and we gawked at him, and I mumbled my "Wanna buy a school candy bar?" pitch to him as he passed into the store, to no effect.

But when he came out, he stopped and chatted for a moment, and he bought a bar, paying five times as much as it cost (and, like most fundraising candy, it cost five times as much as it should to begin with). The Colonel popped it into his bag (which probably held some of the distilled elements of his secret herbs-and-spices recipe), and went on his merry way. As a kid, it was a crowning moment for me. I now like to think of the Colonel in chicken heaven, dropping acid every day, and musing over his chance encounters with youths in front of liquor stores. Incongruous, but funny. At least to me.

Anchoring Your Writing in Place

One of the things that anchors a piece of writing, funny or not, is a sense of place. A feeling of the shape and smell of the terrain, how the light enters and leaves a room, the sag of a roof—those things pull readers in, let them feel the gravity of your work, no matter if it's fiction or non.

A while back, my girlfriend and I were invited to spend the night at a house on the Big Sur coast, a house that my girlfriend's sister was considering buying a shared ownership in. It's a modest home, bringing to mind a style of California hippie houses of the 70s, with funky, unpretentious charm. That comfortable worn-in feeling is both inside and outside the grounds of the home. And then there's the view.

The view, of which the photo above only provides a rather shabby sense of its actual grandeur, is sublime. That's the view you see if you step out the door of the house and move just a bit up the driveway. So, every time I stepped out of that house, my mind shot down that cliff in a delirious riot of color, light, sound and scent. From the cliff, you can hear the ocean whump though the blowholes below, you can hear the trill and squawk of birdsong, you can smell pine and sun-warmed grasses.

Though Big Sur is less than 90 minutes from my house and I too live in a coastal California community, Big Sur is vastly different. It is visually dazzling, with great, craggy cliffs that plunge to a sea crashing on foaming rocks. Even with somewhat recent fires, there are thick forests with trails that lead to rolling waterfalls. There are places like the Henry Miller library, with its eccentric art work in the tree-splashed front yard, the eclectic and thoughtful book collection, the free coffee and Ping-Pong, the absolute "hang out and read a while" feeling of the place. And, while being cautious of stereotyping the locals, Big Sur folks seem friendly in a way that doesn't seem affected.

Place Is a State in Your Reader's Mind

When you are writing about a specific place, you need to open a big window—or step down a short driveway—to the view of that place. But that view must let your reader crunch the gravel underfoot, let them remark on the unusual number of people who have crew cuts, let them peruse a menu that has hush puppies rather than French fries. The setting of my latest novel is mainly the San Francisco of the late 80s, and mostly Market Street downtown. The bike messengers, women in fashionable outfits, ragged homeless and lost tourists of Market Street look, sound and smell different from the people I saw roaming Key West a couple of years ago.

I occasionally go hiking in the redwoods near my house. The redwoods smell different from the pines of Big Sur, they throw the light in a different way from their branches. If you pay real attention to small details that can capture the essence of a place, or distinguish it enough so the reader says, "Ah, so that's what Big

Sur is like," you've gained ground on capturing their imagination too. Or if you can lie skillfully enough to describe the taste of place so that there aren't false notes in the rendering, even if you've never been to that place before, the writing, and the world of imagination it creates, can still hold together.

Oh, about that share in the house: the other partial owners came back, after an absence of some time, to consider whether they really wanted to sell. They came on a beautiful weekend; they decided they couldn't give it up. Damn.

The Twilight Theme

Establishing place can give a tangible, grounded feel to any piece of writing. A less tangible thing is theme, but writing that's filtered through a theme can have a sneaky power.

I'm old enough to have seen *The Twilight Zone* when it was in its regular run on 60s television. I watched it avidly, because it had the perfect composition of creepy/scary/otherworldly that fed and accelerated a kid's imagination. It's only now, having been treated courtesy of the Syfy Channel to a second round of the show, that I recognize what a perfect encapsulation of narrative intrigue the show was and is.

It's a kick to see how many famous actors—Robert Duvall, William Shatner, Dennis Hopper, Robert Redford—added their early panache to the series, which was also notable for rarely straying into the truly cheesy for its special effects, though it was not a big-budget production.

But it wasn't the acting, cinematography or production values that made the show timeless. It was the writing.

Big-Issue Writing Without Schmaltz

The essence of *The Twilight Zone* is in the writing, the inviolate genesis of so mediums that provoke our thinking. And the reason the writing of *The Twilight Zone* was so compelling was that the 30-minute shows were a distillation of the biggest themes of existence: What is the nature of good? What is the nature of evil? How are morals compromised, and why? How can it be that the powerful can be so weak, and the unprepossessing so strong? What is the essence of fear, the power of the unknown? What is death?

Those issues, when spelled out above, can look so sententious, a formula for gloppy entertainment and tasteless treacle. But that's not the case in *The Twilight Zone,* and not the case when those matters, which are serious, are taken seriously. Yet also presented as entertainment, a fine contradiction. And in matters of fine contradiction, the host, creator and prime writer of the series was a master.

Rod Serling, Writer as Philosopher-Magician

Somehow, often using the simplest of language, Rod Serling[35] was able to tap into the well of human nature, finding definitive examples of the pompous and the blustery, the ordinary, the humble, the unassailably good. And though the show could very

---

[35] http://en.wikipedia.org/wiki/Rod_Serling

well tip toward the preachy (against nuclear power, for example), its motions toward advocacy were mostly submerged in the drama. Space exploration could be both the source of enlightenment and destruction. Humans could be more soulless than robots. The spark of creativity, of love, could be found in the most arid of environments.

Rod Serling's consistently good writing was matched by his compelling on-screen persona: the oracular host, biting off words with a steady, clipped, declarative voice that was that of an unequivocal judge, but one always in on the big joke. And the ever-lit cigarette, the smoke wafting into the air like the dashed dreams that so many of the shows depicted. Those cigarettes contributed to ending Serling's life at a cruelly young age, but his legacy is clear: the small man with the big mind and the sonorous voice, still making viewers—and writers—reflect on what it is to be human.

You're traveling through another dimension, a dimension not only of sight and sound but of mind; a journey into a wondrous land whose boundaries are that of imagination. That's the signpost up ahead—your next stop, the Twilight Zone.

Characters, Consistently Inconsistent

Let's move from the *Twilight Zone* to the character zone. Think of your favorite person. Consider all of her fetching qualities: warm heart, intelligence, sense of humor, great, big ... ambitions. Wouldn't it be a bore, though, if that person was consistently, day after long day, the same sterling, one-hundred percent, no-errors-on-the-reference-test creature of righteousness? If that white-winged angel had no cayenne, no quirk that set you off balance, no habit that pulled your eyebrows skyward in scorn—wouldn't that be a metronome-knows-no-change snore?

Might that cause any subsequent favorite person to have a bushelful of appealing qualities too, but also might her favorite music be shredding death metal that makes your eyeballs bleed, but which you find charming in some unfathomable way?

It's the same with characters in fiction. Good characters have the nice eyes, but the five-o'-clock shadow too—there's some cayenne in the popcorn. If you populate your work with ranks of unreservedly good or unconditionally bad citizens, your readers will set the book down in favor of some reality TV, where at least the nice-looking characters are also heroin addicts.

Your Readers, Your Jury

What made me think of those things was a memory from serving on jury duty a couple of years back. What drew my mind toward these dimensions of character was that I first saw the defendant in the case before I'd heard the charges. I had an immediate positive reaction to him: nice smile, good-looking guy, his manner seemed to express some charm. Then I heard the charges read: they were vile. Of course, that's why we have a jury system—there's a presumption of innocence, and the truth must be pursued.

I don't want to discuss the particulars of the case—I simply want to address it in regards to the richness of character development. The trial was, sadly enough, real life. But between the pages, you want your characters to affect your readers emotionally, and often topsy-turvily, as my emotions were affected by the information coming to me in the courthouse.

Those character twistings are why a well-done unreliable narrator can be so interesting. Someone like Raskolnikov in *Crime and Punishment*,[36] who does have many virtues, of passion, of intelligence, but is also mad—mad with ego, mad with violence. (Note: Raskolnikov is technically not the narrator, but we spend much of the time in his fevered head.) Because we are all mixes of emotions and traits, creating characters that are imperfect pulls us in.

The jury work is also a reminder that when you're in an unfamiliar situation, drink it in. Those strange characters and corners of unfamiliar rooms might find a home in a story down the road.

What's the frame for building the consciousness of your fictional characters (and vivid renderings of places where stories unfold)? By gathering both the lunatic and the prosaic blossoms of incident and observation that happen to you over time. As we've established, the hot bricks of story building are everywhere, so bring your wheelbarrow.

Johnny Cash, a True Character

Do you know that Johnny Cash song, "One Piece at a Time"? In it, the song's protagonist works in a Cadillac plant, and he decides

[36] http://en.wikipedia.org/wiki/Crime_and_Punishment

to pilfer car parts to home-build his own Caddy. But because he can only take home one piece at a time, the car takes more than 20 years to build. He does indeed end up with a Cadillac, but as auto fashions—and fins—change greatly over time, his ride is a mongrel. But it's *his* mongrel, uniquely so. That's what you should do with your writing.

No, no, I'm not saying stitch together a Frankensteinian monster with your work, not some particolored pastiche, not Cormac McCarthy's cracked, dry arroyos filled with Danielle Steel's bonneted women fluttering in chiffon. (Do feel free to steal that for your next novel.) What I'm saying is pull from everything you've seen, pull from your life stuff, pull from the bones of your being and from their marrow yet—and put that in your writing.

The premise above might sound like a mouthy way of again saying "write what you know," or maybe even "write what you feel." But it's more along the lines of "write what makes you feel."

The rest of this screed will rely on a pathology known as ODR (Old Dude Reminiscing), but I promise to spill something useful before I have to nap. My pitch is less the knowing that your character would rather have two olives in her martini than one; it's more that as the nosy, observant, judgmental writer that you are, the world has given you endless olives—so employ your toothpick.

Siblings Torture You? Get Even: Write About Them

Let's get into it: it starts at home. When I was about ten, starting to enjoy pop music, my older sister was deep into jazz. Since I couldn't touch her records, when she would leave the house, I'd put on her Hugh Masekela and have my brain cleaved. I didn't like it—I had a visceral "what is this shit?" reaction of dismay and confusion. That boy's mind stutter belongs in a character's mind.

Taking another tack, baseball meant everything to me as an adolescent. I was love-struck by Sandy Koufax, knocked asunder by Willie Mays. I wouldn't have expressed it as such, but what made my eyes glitter was their art, the extraordinary confluence of physical grace and grit, a mastery that yet saw regular failure, because that's baseball. That fan's absorption in a game that produced an indifferent shrug in other people, his blindness to any of his heroes' failings, his overfull heart—that belongs in a character's heart.

Here's a crazy Cadillac fender: for some inexplicable reason, I loved glassware (specifically, drinking glasses) when I was thirteen or so. I liked to go into department stores and look at the wine glasses, the highball glasses. I bought a GIANT brandy snifter, one that a baby could backstroke in, and used it to capture my RC Colas. I'd walk around my house, swirling and sniffing at my drink, while my parents and siblings rolled their eyes. That kid's strange affectations belong in (or on) a character.

Vegas, Bukowski and Funky Texas: Put 'Em In

But let's get out and look around: when I lived in Vegas, I spent a lot of time in casinos. You don't have to look far in Vegas to find funky Cadillac parts in every face, every twitch, every empty pocket. I was sitting outside the Golden Nugget once and a haggard guy came up to me, holding a Mickey Mouse watch in his outstretched hand. "Hey man, give me five bucks for this, it's worth fifty. I just gotta get back to the tables." That guy. That guy, his fractured hope, his Custer's bluster, his canceled ticket—that guy's gutter belongs in a character.

Watching Charles Bukowski read, in a tiny performance house in Huntington Beach when I was a goggle-eyed semi-adult. At various junctures, Bukowski was being harangued by some meathead in the audience, but the poetic crustacean gave back better than he got. However, around Bukowski's 15th beer (he had a cooler of Michelobs on stage), he could only muster a bland "Yeah, well fuck you too" to the guy. Bukowski, wobbly, rheumy-eyed, probably tired of the world's crap before he was even born—put that world-weariness in a character.

I drove around the country years back and took a picture of some beat, closed-down cafe in a funky little town in Texas (not sure what town; might have been WhereInHell), a beautifully ruined joint, probably from the 30s, great arched lines on what looked to be an adobe facade. There was a massive electrical storm miles away I could see lifting the dry dirt. The peeling green paint, the chipped walls, the crackling air, all touched by time's patina—that's a sense of place that should be placed in a book.

Small Moments Writ Large

Small moments have everything too: the woman in the grocery store studying a pickle-jar label for its sodium content, sunglasses pushed up on her head, puzzling at the small letters, suspicious, controlling. Your fellow humans are giving this stuff away, use it. Think of the smashed-up feeling you had after breaking up with someone when you were young—bring that hell to the page. Think of the twist in your heart (well, mine, because I'm petty that way) when another writer has some giant success. That stab and its guilty cousin belong in a book.

I'd like to go on, about the crazy joy I saw in this crazed bootlegger's eye when I went up to his mountaintop aerie to interview him and he showed me his catapult, his small working cannon and the tiny guillotine he had, along with some headless dolls. Book him. I'd also to talk about how my mom's chocolate chip cookies are love, but I've spouted too much already. So, this is just a reminder that we are all grizzled souls with our own Psychobilly Cadillacs. This mean old life will get you one way or another, but grab some of it in passing, and put it in books.

Taking Time and Talking Time

You need to put those characters into books, and fix their britches on the page. Because, like all writers, you have to face time.

Time is a peculiar factor in writers' lives. For all, there is the time when they are not known, tussling with words in obscurity, anxious of an uncertain fate. Then there might be a corona burst of notoriety's light, where the author—often whose 20 years of work belies the falsehood of being termed an "overnight success"—enters a heady phase of fame. Think J.K. Rowling, Elizabeth Gilbert after *Eat, Pray, Love,* Brett Easton Ellis (though in a debut) of *Less Than Zero.* And for some, fame's flare is not a comet that returns, but a thing that sputters and is still again.

And then there is the unsteady—and often unpredictable—rise and fall of fame's tide after an author's death. I suspect that most authors want to leave a legacy, a body of ideas or characters that live on in the public imagination long after the pen or keyboard is stilled. That's phenomena that goes in pulses: you'll have some of Faulkner's works out of print for years, then there might be a Faulkner resurgence, with universities assigning new classes to pick at the authorial bones anew. It's happened with Hemingway and Fitzgerald. Here's a good example: Mark Twain's autobiography, published in 2010, the 100th anniversary of Twain's death.

Can't Get It? It Must Be Good!

Twain was no slouch when it came to marketing. He decreed that his autobiography couldn't be published until 100 years after he lifted off this earthly plane, because he thought that some of the vinegar and piss with which he inked some of his opinions about politics, politicians, public figures and contemporary writers was just too sour. But setting that time restriction on his work created the scarcity factor in the public imagination—wow, this is a time capsule of thunder, surely worth waiting 100 years for!

The University of California Press, the publishers of the work, were somewhat taken aback by the immediate sharp sales of the work, scrambling to meet demand. Or maybe Twain also mandated that the publishers pretend there was a shortage of the volume—that's a tried-and-true technique that his own days as a publisher would have instructed.

The autobiography is a serious work of scholarship, the result of years of research by the Mark Twain Project[37] at UC Berkeley's Bancroft Library. The introduction alone is 63 pages, the explanatory notes in the back more than 200, and the body of the book is in small type. The reason it took a team of scholarly horses to draw Twain's carriage was that the material was like an attic stuffed with oddments, rags, treasures and trifles, and with more works scattered in other literary outbuildings.

Twain began his autobiography innumerable times later in life, and as with many of his writings (*Huckleberry Finn* took more than seven years of on-off writing), dropped the project only to pick it up anew. His first efforts at a more conventional autobiography left him cold. It was only when he came up with the idea of dictating his life story that he moved forward with some vigor. Yet, that capture-the-spoken-word effort too meandered over a course of years, culminating very close to his death.

Fame, Who Needs It? (But Did You Quote Me Accurately?)

Meandered spells it well: Twain didn't settle for a crawling chronology in his dictation, but approached it in the manner of one of his storyteller's speeches: He chose a subject to speak about, and played it out in his mind and then his mouth, as he

---

[37] http://www.marktwainproject.org

lay in bed (where a good deal of the dictation was done). Thus the work is a series of impressions, sketches, anecdotes, and profiles, at kin with the range of his lifetime's body of works. So the autobiography is a crazy-quilt of stitching and sorting; it would undoubtedly amuse Mr. Clemens to know that it took over 200 pages of annotations to set the story straight (or less crooked, as it were). And this is only volume one! The second volume came out three years later, at 776 pages, and I haven't taken that one on, because I haven't been eating enough protein. I believe one more is planned, unless crafty Twain had another trove of scribblings that he deemed so scurrilous that they could only be released 200 years after his death.

I read a book of collected letters between Jack Kerouac and Allen Ginsberg detailing their pre-fame literary efforts and crestfallen declarations over ever being published. The letters have an almost overwrought flailing of despair and delight. At one point, after Ginsberg had his seminal *Howl* published, he began getting the attention that he'd craved. There had been an article in the New York Times that had discussed the poem and the poet, and Ginsberg referenced that article in a letter to Kerouac, saying, "Agh! I'm sick of the whole thing, that's all I think about, famous authorhood, like a happy empty dream."

To my mind, a "happy empty dream" seems like an apt description of fame. But maybe I'm tasting grapes gone sour—or something that will taste like wine over time. Oh well, at least I have the Twain tattoo.

Time and Twinkies Wait for No Man (Women Either)

I don't want to finish up about writing and time without bringing up a natural connection: Twinkies.

I'd like for you to think of your writing as Twinkies—not for its abysmal nutritive content, but for the extraordinary vitality of its preservative army: your writing can continue marching on, even after it has bivouacked for a while. Twinkies, of course, have a reputation for staying soft and squeezy long past their recommended consumption date (if anyone recommends consuming Twinkies). Such is the less-sugary substance of your writing—you can achieve successes with writing that has been gathering hard-drive webs, by sending it out anew after its slumber. You can also redirect writing that you thought was a fruit, but really turned out to be a vegetable. (Note: Twinkies are not vegetables. Or fruits.)

Here's what I mean: A couple of years ago I received an email telling me that I'd won a scholarship to the Wrangling with Writing conference in Tucson, Arizona. The award, which included the hotel room and some meals, was given to me on the strength of an essay I wrote long before that—not for this conference, but for another online contest. Though the topic of the conference essay was pretty close to the online contest essay, I had to trim out some fat and slant it a touch to make it fit their guidelines. I really didn't think I'd win, but I had the piece snoozing on my hard drive, so why not wake it from its nap?

Slot Machines on Ice: Melt Them

Another roll of the dice: years ago, I wrote a short story about Las Vegas[38] set in the 70s. I'd prodded and poked that thing a bunch of times, sending it out to magazines and small literary publications. No jackpot. So, it sat with its slot machine unplugged for a while until I thought, what the heck—I sent it out years later to *The Labletter,*[39] and they were happy to publish (and pay for) it in in their annual journal of arts and literature.

And just one more example of how you can shave the grizzled beard of your writing to reveal the fresh face below. I wrote a short story in grad school about some high school shoplifting hijinks (alluded to earlier) that was never published. Years later, I heard about the National Steinbeck Center's short story contest. I thought it was a real long shot, but again, why not? I was shocked to have won, and still cherish the lovely glass plaque that was given to me. I cherished the $1,000 prize as well.

Naturally, I haven't emphasized the bajillions of rejections I've received over time for my Tantric poetry muffin recipes, or that little matter of the novel that can't seem to fit in any agent's ear. But I don't need to emphasize those, because they don't matter. What matters is that you can't succeed if you don't keep sending the stuff out. Once in a while, those old Twinkies will still have a twinkle.

---

[38] http://www.tombentley.com/Highway.pdf

[39] http://www.labletter.com

Bonus Twinkies Story

Many years ago when I lived in Seattle, I dated a nice woman whose high apartment windows faced out on a warehouse district in the city. One late evening, staring out at the cityscape, I notice some huge trucks—with big cylindrical carriers like gasoline trucks use—lined up against a factory building, with giant chutes attached. When I asked my pal what was going on, she said that those were sugar trucks, and that they were unloading their white wonder into the Twinkie factory!

Since I have been a lifelong fan of sugared objects, that gave me quite a thrill, and it was rather a hallucinatory sight to witness the eerie glow from the wee-hour factory lights, dumping massive amounts of sugar in the semi-darkness, destined to torque the brains of young children all over America. There was something criminally poetic about it all ...

Your Old Writing, Born Anew

Talking about time and writing, if you have written for a while, you intimately know the combination of puzzlement and horror that happens when you read something you'd written years back. But sometimes you can see the sparks of what brought you to writing in the first place. Because I just can't be direct about this, let's use a bird as my muse.

There are lots of mockingbirds in my neighborhood. In spring, every morning for at least a month, a mockingbird will rise with winged purpose to the top of the telephone pole nearest our house. From there, he will release an unbridled enthusiasm of trills, tweets and thrilling cascades of notable notes, seemingly of endless variation. I have read that a mockingbird can sing more than 400 different songs; I like to think that my mockingbird was Sinatra in feathers—400 songs is just a morning's work, and the evening calls for 400 more.

But what I really like to think is that the mockingbird was unleashing a torrent of stories, rapid-fire, almost like a stand-up comedian. They are all colorful and antic: "Hey, do you remember the time I dated a blue jay? That ended so badly that every time I see a bird dressed in blue I head south for the winter." And that story is then followed by a quick tale of why warblers make the best therapists and on.

Stories are fascinating; well-told, they pull a listener forward, with a "And then what happened? No way!" or "Don't tell me anymore, that's too sad. But did she die?" When a story clicks, all the elements—place, plot, character, mood—coalesce into a miniature world, a world where you feel the light breezes, and cower from the heavy storms.

Can My Tales Carry a Tune?

I had a story collection *Flowering and Other Stories*[40] released by a small press, AM Ink, in early 2012. Working with the company's editor for a couple of months was interesting, because many of the stories were older pieces, written in the 80s and 90s. Revisiting them was like perching on a telephone pole from quite a ways off—the writer that sang those stories isn't quite the writer I

[40] http://www.amazon.com/Flowering-Other-Stories-Tom-Bentley/dp/0984580174

know now, though many a turn of phrase still fits in the ear. There are some newer pieces in there too, but the bulk of them are from some time back.

What was particularly intriguing in the edit was that for a couple of stories I was requested to make modest-yet-significant changes to the endings. I had considered those stories fixed, but in working on them again, I see they are more like songs: stretching a note, slowing the cadence, pushing the melody—a change in rhythm is a change in meaning. Most gratifying is that I think the editor made good suggestions and that the work has been improved.

PS I understand that the male mockingbird sings his springtime stories to attract a mate; if my girlfriend asks, tell her I'm only doing the book to please my mother.

Ending with an Edit

Why don't we round out this section with some words on editing.

And on potatoes.

Let's consider a nice serving of mashed potatoes, hot and buttery. Most cooks probably don't think too much about preparing their potatoes, so it's often a rote task, hurried through to get to the entree. But what if those potatoes were served with panache, with some kind of style point or spicy twist? Say you were served potatoes with a tiny derby hat on them. You'd remember those spuds, wouldn't you?

You'd probably remember them even more, if under the tiny derby was a clump of hair. Wouldn't that clump drag what was an interesting expression of creativity into an unappetizing corner? The reason I bring up potatoes, odd hats and unwanted hair is a point I want to make about editing. Competent editors are able to shape the standard serving of potatoes so that it's without lumps, smooth and palatable. Good potatoes, but still just potatoes.

Better editors recognize when a piece of writing has a derby hat in it—they would never take that hat out, robbing the writer of a unique angle or voice. They'd find a way to allow the hat to fit snugly in its potato surroundings, fully expressive of its quirk and charm, without it seeming unnatural or foreign. And of course, a good editor would remove that hair—typos, kludgy expressions, dully passive voice, et al—posthaste.

Seeing What's Missing from the Plate

Another skill possessed by a good editor is recognizing when something's missing. If you don't provide the reader with a fork, they can't fully enjoy those potatoes. Some pieces of writing are strong, but they might have gaps in logic, or need to be buttressed by a few more starchy facts. Good editors notice if the writing meal is missing ingredients, and they know how to persuasively suggest adding them so that the writer chefs promptly step back up to the stove.

Of course, editors should always recognize when that potato serving is too big. I remember one of my first copywriting jobs out of college, writing catalog copy for an outdoor equipment retailer that sold a lot of camping goods. One of our products was the

Backpacker's Bible, which was a tiny book that gathered some of the most powerful/popular Bible verses (no "begats" allowed). My first round of copy for it had the line, "The best of The Book, with all the deadwood cut away." [Note: for some odd reason they didn't use my copy.]

And editors recognize when something's just off. If you're serving your potatoes to Lady Gaga, you don't want her wearing her octopus-tentacle bra tinted some neutral shade of grey, do you? It cries out to be Day-Glo puce!

If writing has a certain rhythm established, and the rhythm, without context, goes awry, a good editor will re-establish that rhythm. And the proper bra color.

Editing Flavors

Editing a book-length project is an intriguing undertaking for the sheer variety of the material an editor might see. I've edited both fiction and nonfiction works for years, having cut my eyeteeth on big software manuals (the writing of which can be more creative than might be imagined) long years ago, and having advanced into novels and nonfiction projects as time's train moved on. I'm editing a long (and winningly crazy) science-fiction novel right now.

In this universe and its parallel ones, you'll find some argument as to what an editor specifically does ("slash the soul out of an artist's heart" might be one angle) and divergent discussion yet about the types of editing. But I set up my lemonade stand with three: developmental editing, copyediting (or line editing) and proofing. You could stack a lot of words to describe the distinctions—and other editors break them down into more categories yet—but for this discussion, let's call developmental editing the big-picture shakeout.

Consider how you might assess a nonfiction work for its structure: does it have a solid foundation, are the walls of its ideas well-framed, does the front door open to the living room rather than the bathroom, does the roof of its concepts leak, are the floors of its logic cracked?

In fiction, sometimes one of the developmental editor's jobs might be simply to make the author consider if a character's gesture or expression is really the one the author intended, to introduce the idea that on the fundamental sentence and word level can rest the lasting power of the work. But more often the developmental editor's job might be to question whether a character even *belongs* in the work. Asking an author to consider such a heavy structural issue (such a question should only be part of a developmental edit, to be sure) is asking a lot—but sometimes those questions need to be asked. And you as an author have every latitude to just say no. (or, Hell No!)

You get much more granular with a line edit, inspecting paragraphs and sentences for diction, flow, grammar and clarity: is the expression of the espoused ideas crisp, clean, cliché-free? Do verbs have verve? Does a subject play hide and seek with its predicate so that even a sugary gingerbread trail of subordinate clauses can't lead the way home to understanding?

Those Lowly Chimney Sweeps

Proofreaders might be considered the lowly chimney sweeps of the editing ranks, but if your work is blackened by misspellings, typos, transposed words/letters, extra words, you'll want their cleansing touch. So many times I'll see a stray "a" next to an "an," or an "is is" that makes for an *is not*. Or inconsistency of usage and style—writing "versus" when it's been "vs" all along. Such soot means the book's fire just won't burn clean. And sometimes a work will need an extra sweeping, because when initial errors are corrected, new errors are introduced. (Which should be some kind of law, like the Verbiage Uncertainty Principle.)

And my mom wanted me to be a brain surgeon. She just didn't realize that editors are pretty much surgeons too. And sometimes politicians. And psychologists. And—oh, don't get me started. (So, gentle readers, can you now answer the burning question: "What's an Editor Do Besides Unnecessarily Charge You?")

If that question's not distracting enough, let's move on to a whole chapter on writing distractions (and some cures).

6

Writing Distractions and Their Discontents

In this section of the book, let's discuss how to make your writing moments count, and observe (and revile!) the discouragements and distractions that can draw you away from the counting. First, I want to go through some of the negative thought processes that can freeze your progress as a writer, using my own examples as a caution. Some of these revelations might seem those of a slipshod bumbler (what did you call me?), but they're here because I've experienced where you can get in your own way as a writer, and give some suggestions on how to climb over that prostrate form and type again.

A simple example: I know so well how much can be accomplished by the simple and doable task of writing for a half-hour every day—I finished a long slumbering novel that way. But I also know how the monkey mind can find beckoning bananas around every corner, and can make you drop the keyboard so quick you'll forget where you left it.

But First, Art's Soothing Siren

But before we muck our boots in the mire, let's rise up; let's muse about some of art's inspirations. We need some lift before we hit the basement.

For a long time, I've kept a torn-out, short magazine piece on my refrigerator. It's a discussion by the photographer Harold Feinstein[41] about life and art. I try to read it every once in a while to remind myself that amidst all of the crap that is daily life, amidst the detritus of the mind, its self-deceits and rationalizations and wastes, there is something more.

Here are some quotes from the Feinstein piece that say it better: *"My formal education began and ended in kindergarten. Just give me paints, and clay and crayons and blocks and reams of paper—and someone who loves what I do. At age seven, when I discovered there was something called an 'artist," it was an epiphany. I thought, 'You mean you can just do this?'*

"When, at age 15, I looked through the viewfinder of my neighbor's Rolleiflex, I had another epiphany. Everything looked like a photograph, and it was easy. This is what I loved about it. We don't trust that which comes with ease; instead we tend to complicate everything. My family was disappointed, 'Can't you stick with anything?' That was 53 years ago. I guess I can."

[41] http://www.haroldfeinstein.com/bio/

We Were Born Wise and Taught To Be Stupid

"I believe we were born wise and taught to be stupid ... we have become info-maniacs. We confuse technique with the accumulation of massive amounts of technological data. Good technique is that which interferes least with the voice of our soul ... The conditioning we confuse with education teaches us to defer our vision to an outside authority, without respect for the authority within.

Somehow we come to believe that 'art' lies on some mountain or museum beyond our reach, that we are indeed impostors at the door of art.

... it is astounding how difficult it is for people to accept and believe perceptive compliments without in some way discounting them. Art is an affirmation. If we are afraid that some of our images will reveal us as fools, or at least as inadequate for the journey, we will never discover our brilliance."

Yeah. What he said.

And let's savor a quote from that wise woman, Annie Dillard:[42] "How we spend our days is, of course, how we spend our lives."

Make 'em count.

---

[42] http://www.anniedillard.com/

Writing Passionately (Or, Garcia Looked Right at Me, Dude)

Long ago, a hundred bad haircuts into my Jurassic past, I regularly attended Grateful Dead concerts. I went to a lot of them, because for me and a zillion other fervid fans, the Dead could get us off, riding a mass-mind and bouncing-body electric-rhythm rocket, unlike any other band. When the Dead were crackling, they had the audience bonded in an escalating excitement of communal glee. Sure, it might have been the acid, but I actually was courageous enough to occasionally attend Dead concerts where I *didn't* take acid, and that you-had-to-be-there effect was still pronounced: a shared sense of good times and collective conviviality that seems completely corny when I try to describe it now.

One of the amusing side notes of being among the ragged clowns that tagged after the Dead train was that during one of Jerry Garcia's piquant, extended guitar noodlings, there would invariably be among the crowd of bliss kittens a guy who would turn, a Saul-at-Damascus look in his eyes, and gush to whomever was listening, "Jerry, looked right at me! We connected, man! Did you see it?" And for the rest of the concert, the fellow touched by the divine was just a little higher than anyone else, if that was possible.

I directly heard variants of that statement many times, and read the same long years later in concert reviews online, when one of the faithful described the moment that lifted him. (And note: this was always a man that staked this claim—the women seemed content to merely twirl in the tantalizing twists of sound.)

Though I always played on the periphery of the true believers, and was caught up many times in the glow of the groove, I never could climb to the top of that ladder, where Garcia's gown glimmered—my articles of faith always needed editing. I've always marveled at the faith that people have, in a God described to them from pages written lifetimes ago, faith in the depth of their abilities, however limited or constrained by evidence, faith in the certainty that Garcia looked right at them, man.

As far as I can remember, I've been uncomfortable, or perhaps jealous of, deep expressions of faith and certainty in people and in movements, because there seems so much contingency and randomness in life. And because faith seemed so exclusionary of fact. But that's the nature of faith, isn't it?

Keeping the Faith (or Trying to Locate It)

This is a long-winded way of saying that I go in and out of phase in my writing conviction. I've become accustomed to the stints of mild depression I've experienced for many years, watching them and waiting them out, because they do always lift, though some phases last longer than others. It's easy to get indulgent with our pains—"No, I couldn't possibly write that essay today, I'm in a bad mood." Bad moods can be useful delaying tactics.

Sometimes, when you are deep in your own head, that sense of "what's the use of writing" can seem like all you've got. But the pain of writing disappointment is nothing compared to real emotional pain. I was reminded of that when I listened to a radio broadcast of interviews with wounded vets who were learning how to ride bicycles after their limbs had been blown off. All of them were expressing such an eagerness to move forward with the difficult therapy and complex equipment that would bring them back to the simple pleasure of riding a bike.

Suffering does unite us, but hearing of suffering that seems leagues beyond your own serves as a good reality check. Those soldiers had faith they'd ride the bikes again; they were committed to doing the work to make it happen. It's a different kind of faith than the intangible one I struggled with as an altar boy, trying to discern just when and how a little bit of flour could be transformed into the body of Christ by a priest's declaration. I was always more interested in trying some of the sacramental wine.

Sharing the Feeling (the Vomit Stains Are Extra)

I said earlier that suffering unites us, but as Tolstoy says in *Anna Karenina,* "Happy families are all alike; every unhappy family is unhappy in its own way." At intervals, my own way has been to be stuck, faithless in my head, but that should always mean it's time to get on the bike, get the kinks out, try and write without too much judgment.

But before the ride, one more concert story: I was at a Hot Tuna concert in L.A. back in my salad days. There was a break between sets where people were milling about in that hive-like concert way. I was sitting down on the floor, a ways from the stage. For some reason, my eyes lit on a fellow who was a fair distance away, wobbling and lurching about like he was very drunk. I idly watched him making a circuitous route through the crowd, probably keeping my eyes on him for several minutes.

His wanderings finally took him to a spot directly in front of me, whereupon he unloaded a rich stream of vomit on the floor, with a fair amount landing on my pants. It wasn't pleasant at the time, but the memory always makes me laugh, because I contrast it with the other concert experience of "Jerry looked at me!"

At least Jerry didn't vomit on me. Keep the faith.

No Tomorrow in Writing?

Hope I haven't made you question your own writing conviction yet, because I want to expand on the theme of there being no tomorrow in your writing, and that sounds precipitous too. Before the expansion, there's the short version: get it said today. Or at least write the first sentence.

I sent an email to Nelson Mandela a while before he died, asking him for an interview. These are interesting times—if you poke around a bit, you can often find a listed email address for all kinds of folks. Of course, the address I found for Mr. Mandela was probably one handled by a phalanx of administrative types who send most requests down a tube into large cellar vats, to be boiled with the suet and other table scraps. (These are likely the same functionaries who dispatch my queries to the *New Yorker* into a similar large vat of innocuous fats.)

But DOA queries aren't my point here; my point is that if you don't take the initiative to further your writing career, who will? If you have been sitting on an essay about your cousin Doreen who drained the family bank accounts, joined a Mexican drug cartel and now owns a quarter of the blood diamond trade in Liberia because you were squeamish about the family reaction, when *will* you write it? Every writing thought that isn't written is just evaporated water.

I edited the memoirs of a woman who is in her mid-sixties, and it's provocative stuff: the political tumult of the San Francisco Bay Area 1960s and 1970s, filtered through the view of a rebellious coming-of-age adolescent who experienced a dizzying amount of personal roller-coastering. Lots of torquing family entanglements, including affairs, alienation and death. Even though many of the principals are still alive, she knew that she had to put the truth on the page—this is her chance to tell the story, and she's not sparing feelings, including her own.

Fate Is Indifferent to the Closing of Doors

Now that my once-dark locks are streaked with grey, it's become more clear to me that I have to write as though there were no tomorrow. Because there isn't—you just don't know fate's hand. I see among my own friends and family where fate has closed doors on people who presumed they'd be long open. I've mentioned my father's Alzheimer's—before he was fully swathed in the fabric of that disease, he was a decent storyteller. For the last couple of his years, he could still shakily—and almost randomly—utter clear thoughts, but he could no longer command language. I realize now how little I actually knew of him—and didn't have the sense or gumption to ask. I saw stories locked in my father's eyes, but they were his stories, not mine—and now he can't tell them.

I don't want to be morbid, just realistic. One good car crash can make "what might have been" the saddest song, or you can just peter out your time, thinking there's bushels of it to waste. I have been a big procrastinator in my writing life, loving literature, but rarely writing passionately. Books and stories published here and there, a fair chunk of articles, but I never felt *driven* to write, as I've read of some authors. Passionate at times about language, and in love with lyrical expression, but driven? No.

I found one of the strongest messages of Seth Godin's rousing book, *Linchpin,*[43] to be this: *Don't settle. Do your best work.* If not now, when? Take some risks. If you fail, so be it. At least you acted, moved the pieces on the chessboard, ate the cake instead of agonizing over its calories, said "I'm for this!" instead of "Someday, I might be for that."

Oh yeah—if you happen to talk to Nelson Mandela in a séance, tell him I'm waiting for an answer.

Could That Melancholy Come in On a Winter Writer's Wind?

A wind has blown the rain away and blown the sky away and all the leaves away, and the trees stand. I think, I too, have known autumn too long.

—e.e. cummings

I have some measure of SAD, that aptly named Seasonal Affective Disorder, where the shorter days and the dimming light seem to drain my batteries. Spring is here now (and miraculously, there was a bit of rain last week, in drought-dry California. But I

[43] http://www.amazon.com/Linchpin-Are-Indispensable-Seth-Godin/dp/1591843162/

want to talk about winter first, in discussing a writer's seasons. In winter here, the sun does struggle forward as the day turns, but effort is fitful, the results tenuous. The change to the darker months always provokes melancholy in me. It's a host of things: the winds pick up a bit, and their whispers are cooler; they curl under my collar, with cold intent. Leaves dry and curl, lose vitality and color, and fall brittle to the ground. The light itself, its weak slant, its ebbing warmth, seems a conspiracy. Or even a taunting: time rolls on, what have you done?

But whatever the physical component of that, whatever the tangible indicators of time's timeless march, there's a kind of surrender to the conspiracy that's purely psychological. After all, fall is a time of harvest, often one of fruition. Winter can have a mellowing, contemplative effect. (And of course, I live in California, where folks of the Eastern flavor would make a scornful roll of the eyes at whimperings from a body that's never touched a snow shovel.) And yet, and yet, there's always the feeling for me at fall's outset that the movement is toward winter, and that spring won't come again. I've looked at fall as an ending, rather than a beginning.

There's Really Not An Effing Thing to Whinge About

But I'm making the effort to be more conscious of my moods, and look at them with a sort of dispassionate affection: "Oh, a bit on the whiny side today, are we? Maybe it's just a nap after lunch that's needed, or a quick go-round with a neighbor's cow and the trebuchet." Partially because I've been trying to put one of the tenets of a book I read, *Buddha's Brain*, into practice. One of its many salubrious offerings is to recognize that there is the situation, and then there is your reaction to the situation. I know, old porridge that, but the book offers a number of approaches to recognize that when the elements of your nervous system light their alarms and dispense their flight/fight/brain-blight chemicals, you can consciously pour on a cerebral cocktail of your own making to soften the assault.

Thus we have the winter, here and ahead. Instead of thinking of the next Ice Age, I can think of my next birthday, the sympathetic shape of pumpkins, the writing conference I'm soon to attend, and good soup. When fall turns towards winter, I get that little shiver of apprehension.

Better to take to heart Samuel Butler, who said, "Youth is like spring, an over praised season more remarkable for biting winds than genial breezes. Autumn is the mellower season, and what we lose in flowers we more than gain in fruits."

One way to taste fruit anew (and tingle your writer's mind) is to simply move. My girlfriend and I often drive down to Big Sur, one of God's palaces on earth. Take the top down on the Miata, hike around a winding hillside overlook with waves crashing on rocks below, go to the sweetly eccentric Henry Miller Library,[44] where you can fondle the Ginsbergs and the Kerouacs, flipped through their old vinyl records from decades past, envy the giant coon cat sleeping on the warm deck, eat a scrumptious lunch high on the hill at Ventana, and came home dizzy with sun.

Here's a perspective I wish I could perpetually renew:

---

[44] http://www.henrymiller.org

In the depth of winter I finally learned that there was in me an invincible summer.

—Albert Camus

Gratitude. Why Didn't I Think of That?

And there are always things to be grateful for:

First, I'm still grateful to remain above ground. I don't know what's on the menu in eternity, but for the moment, I'm dieting. I'm happy there are hummingbirds, old friends, cake and metaphors. And let's hear it for words: there are gallons of them about, but I'll never tire of the drinking. Words have weight, and they are often slung about carelessly; I've got some flesh wounds myself from both delivering and darting away from them, but they still provide me with comfort.

And it seems to me that there's never been a better time to be a freelance writer, whether you're in it for the shekels or the soulfulness. For example, as mentioned earlier, in this past two years, I've spent a month in Panama and two in the Bahamas, and three weeks in Mexico, only because the Internet's indulgences let me ply my trade many meaty miles from where the trading was done.

I'm an accomplished complainer, but I'm trying to be happy with the little things. For instance, my sideburns are coming in nicely. After all, look what Faulkner's mustache did for him. Look what Gertrude Stein's mustache—well, never mind. But finding small pleasures is bigger than it seems.

The Keyboard Reels at the Possibilities

So, here in 2016, I might try writing an advice column for the lovelorn, using only passages from Dickens. For instance, his "Cows are my passion. What I have ever sighed for has been to retreat to a Swiss farm, and live entirely surrounded by cows," might work well for someone hoping to leave an office affair.

Or maybe a write a cookbook of Dali's favorite foods. His favorite drink was said to be a cocktail made of absinthe and eggs. Perhaps add some melted watch and cheese, and a bowler hat full of similes. You get the idea—the coming year is wide open.

For those of you who do sometimes succumb to the thoughts that the writing life isn't worth the trouble, I have some words. (Writers and their weapons!) I want to wrap up the mope session I started in the pages above with some thoughts about the rewards of the writing work.

Strawberry season has begun again, here on the California coast. For months out of the year, I can walk around my neighborhood or drive back from a beach and see fields filled with pickers, backs bent, boxes at their side. Because I live right across from acres of strawberries, the labors of the laborers aren't far from my mind.

Here in my home office, a box of another sort—a computer—defines my workspace. I bend over the keyboard, straightening when the consciousness of ergonomic violation rings in my brain—or in my back. I have the luxury of being able to look out of my yard at the pickers, and to look back into the window of my screen, and think about the nature of work.

I've been a freelancer for many years now, and I should be accustomed to the harvest of my vocation. But it still seems odd to me that this gossamer fruit—an electronic window painted with language—is what I exchange for my daily bread. It seems so removed from "real" work, work that results from your body's toil, or work that produces a tangible thing.

It's easy to scorn this slant, which has a seeming smack of the patronizing in it—sure, here's a guy who gets to sit at home all day, drumming up some artificial envy for work that is ill-paid—and that sometimes results in ill workers. But there's something about the substance of work done by the motion of the body that has a different kind of reward than that done by the motions of the mind. Admittedly, it's a luxury to be in the position to even ponder the differences.

The Bricks and Mortar of Creative Connection

I think my true worker's envy might be toward those people that can build things, and touch them after the building. That process seems a true creative connection, a thing conceived and then a thing concrete. It has to be a pleasure to be a carpenter who passes by houses or buildings he or she has worked on, and who can say, "I made that." I've always been amazed by people that can build, whether it's a cabin or cabinet.

As I mentioned early in this book, I'll always be grateful to my mother, who taught me the love of reading, and my father, who taught me the love of athletics, and to the both of them for revealing that the world can provoke laughter. However, my upbringing didn't urge that craftsperson's understanding, where your fingers gain a native appreciation for constructing the objects of this world. I didn't pick up the building skills that many kids learned—and I didn't go out and learn them on my own. I'm much better with a dishtowel than a hammer. In work as in play, it does seem we're all jealous of the other person, but if it's any consolation, they're probably jealous of us.

Many are the times that I've griped about not hearing back from an editor on a story pitch, or tugged hard on my hair when I can't bring to life on the page a character that shines in my mind. However, it takes some real effort to credibly mope over most aspects of my own vocation. I hope it's not some lame wishful thinking to think of working with words as a kind of carpentry: stories are crafted of words, the hammers and nails that build a tale. Some stories have strong joints, some weak. All stories have foundations, good and bad. There's pleasure in seeing a story's sinews, running your mind's eye over its rough spots, calculating how much more cement is needed to settle a paragraph.

Writing Has Its Harvests Too

Here in the low hills, the strawberry-picking season moves forward; there are workers in the fields, filling boxes from the new plantings. I wonder if the same workers will return again for next year's berries, if they look forward to another season of these pretty hills and ocean breezes. Or if it's just all backbreaking drudgery, surrounded by stories of Silicon Valley successes, which boggle the imaginations of people sweating to stay alive.

I hope not. I still remember my own forays into orchard labor, from many summers of picking apples. So long ago, but I still carry the memory of the crisp explosion of flavor and the sharp gratification gained from munching orchard apples at 6am at the beginning of a long summer day. It's hard to forget the tang of homemade applesauce made for the first time, and the fine feeling I had picking the final apple of a harvest season. But I knew it was only another summer's labor, and that my future didn't lie in those trees. Other workers aren't so lucky. I hope the strawberry workers still feel some satisfaction in those long workdays, and that the strawberries still taste sweet.

I'll try to look more for the writing berries, and to remember to savor the labor.

On an Island, Even the Stones Sing

I hope that me recounting instances of my stepping in writing poop isn't tiring or boring. There are a couple more tales that are instructive of cleaning that poop off your shoe:

Eleven years ago, I lived for a year on a tiny Micronesian island, as I mentioned. I taught various English department classes to students at the junior college, and for several reasons, my stay there was flavored with some sour stints of depression and anxiety. But I like to think about the things there that soothed me: the extraordinary beauty of the waters, the dazzling, resplendent corals and marine life under that water, the tropical breezes that lightened the blazing hammer of the days.

But one of the things I remember so clearly is a sound (maybe because they didn't have any of Proust's madeleines there with which to tag my aroma memory). That sound was the bright, high, rattling tinkle of waves breaking and receding over the bits and chunks of coral at the water's edge. There was a broad coral reef surrounding the island, and there was coral rubble of all shapes and sizes at the shoreline.

When the waves brushed over that coral, it was as though a master—and eccentric, maybe like Thelonious Monk—pianist or perhaps a vibrant vibes player finger-danced over coral keys.

It's challenging to describe a sound, particularly one that because of the variable tempo of the waves and the configuration of the coral was forever changing, but there was something so pleasingly calming about it; the repetitive sweep of the waves and its tinkling chime was an aural massage. After some particularly crappy days at the school, just coming back to our house and sitting by the ocean listening to the jangling chime of the coral was enough to bathe my bile in a sonic balm.

No Coral Concert? Just Breathe Instead

I bring up those island days because this chapter is circling the wagons of those biting bouts of writing anxiety and depression. But there are things that extinguish any flaming arrows. I've found some ways to relieve that sense (and that sense is often just an unreliable voice in your head) that your writing work is not accomplished, that it's not delivering on its promise.

I can conjure many reasons not to write: worrying that a button was missing off my shirt, wondering if that girl from high school really didn't like me or just slashed my tires to get my attention, thinking I would work on my novel if there weren't a section of the tax code online I should study for an hour or two—the list knows no end. No writers need to add "I feel like a deflated tire" to the long list of inanities that prevent them from applying the magic formula: put the time in, and the words will come.

So, for the past year and a half, I've started the morning with a simple meditation. I'm not going to get militantly woo-woo on you and tell you that you have to do 1,000 Sun Salutes, an hour of chanting and then stare at the sun until God speaks, and that then your writing will flow like the mighty river. What I'm doing is simple: a 15- or 20-minute meditation that has been working for me like the sweet sound of waves on coral: a lightly stirred serving of *now*, and now again. This particular meditation is a guided one, though you certainly don't need an iPad to sit and breathe. This guidance is served up by a modulated woman's voice offering some thoughts on focusing on the present moment, then offering silence, then focusing on the ebb and flow of the breath, then silence, and on.

And it's helping.

Breathing Through the Ping-Pongings of Your Infernal Mind

The meditation suggests that you look with kindness on the ping-pongings of your infernal mind, that mad monkey that goes from, "Are we low on milk" to "If the asteroid hits and destroys the earth in a week, I won't have to make the payment on the flat-screen TV." Beginning my morning with a simple meditation, and reminding myself that any time throughout the day, I can return to a minute or two of acknowledging the rolling ride of my breath (rather than watch another YouTube video) has been liberating in some ways.

I bookend the meditation with some quick thoughts on things I'm grateful for. And these don't have to be any complex or grandiose or self-aggrandizing things, like being grateful for the Apple stock split. No, it's more like the "I'm grateful for the sound of waves on coral." Ahhhhh ...

My feeling about my writing has been better—it's breathing some new life. And I'm doing a little more of it. I wish I'd found out earlier that writing is actually a breathing exercise.

Stories Drop from the Sky (But Sometimes I Forget to Reach Out)

Sometimes in that meditation, I lose that restrictive sense of self (or obsession with self that often seems to trip me up) and just settle in. I think those "empty" states are kind of the compost heap of the mind, where in the quiet goop, good things stew and brew. Stories, even.

There is something about beginnings and endings that makes me pull out my wise sage hat. Nope, I'm not going to (at least immediately) discuss how to begin and end a story, because sages ever so much wiser than me have blithered on that more persuasively than I ever will. (By the way, I've always found "Mother died today. Or maybe yesterday; I can't be sure," from Camus' *The Stranger* a beginning that ropes me in.)

Here's the part where I get all writer-like and such: I'd been mulling over writing a certain short story for a couple of years. The premise is dark and fascinating, but I just didn't have a way in.

I couldn't "hear" the point-of-view the story should be told from, didn't have an footing for an opening. So, I figured that was a fertile idea that had withered and died.

But then, Zeus or Buddha or Hunter Thompson decided to throw a random bolt at me. A couple of days ago, the idea for the story rose up again, and I quickly sketched out an opening setting for the story, the main point-of-view character, and some plot points. Why now, after mulling and dropping it for two years? Why?

Well, it's like the plums that appear in my yard from that tree I mentioned that's ancient, severely cracked at the trunk, and that for part of the year appears dead. Then the tree produces the sweetest plums I've ever had. I take it as an act of grace. I have no idea what that tree will do next year—maybe it will have avocados. But I'm grateful for the harvest, of both those juicy plums and the juicy frame of that story.

Now I just have to write. Stories just don't blossom without words.

Writing Ebbs and Flows, and Motivational Triggers

Let's discuss how getting lost in your writing is actually getting found.

I recently entered a travel-writing contest. Normally, I'm pretty balanced about deadlines and details, but I'd let some things pile up, so I only had one day to write the contest entry. I did know the direction I wanted the piece to go, so I dove in. For some people, deadline demand is keyboard caffeine: it's only when the threat of an editor's talons or a manager's teeth is near that production ramps up. I'm better when I have a more measured command of the deadline, when I can pool-cue ideas around to see in which pockets they sink, when I can return to a work in progress and let its established path move me forward.

Instead, lunatic typing to meet this deadline. When I judged I was about one-third of the way through the piece, I revisited the submission site to make sure I had all the facts straight. Nope. The contest had a 1,200-word restriction; I was already at 1,100 words. Gack! My first thought was to abandon this contest—I needed WAY more space to develop the ideas in this piece. And I knew how hard it would be to condense those ideas, as well as re-work the existing material to fit in the smaller space. My thoughts, in essence: "Ugh!"

But I was already at the keyboard, so for the next couple of hours, I worked that story, snipping where snipping was due, expanding where there was a loose fold in the lines. The upshot is that I was able to put together a credible entry. But the uppitiest upshot was that in that phase of cutting and crafting, I was really lost in the work. I rarely get in that state of flow[45]—as it's so compellingly elucidated by Mihaly Csikszentmihalyi—that I felt its appealing allure. [Note: C's name can be used to stop crimes in progress:

[45] http://en.wikipedia.org/wiki/Flow_(psychology)

just shout it at the perpetrators at the top of your lungs.]

The Goldilocks Challenge: It Ain't About Hair Products

As Daniel Pink so convincingly explains in *Drive,* his great book on motivation, we need the Goldilocks challenge: something not too easy, but not too hard: something that challenges us just right. And when we get those challenges, our reward is intrinsic—the task is its own reward. Lately, I've spent some time considering narrowing my range of services, and I had been considering removing book-length editing (I edit both nonfiction work and fiction) from the list, thinking it secondary to my copywriting work.

But I realized from my travel-essay edit how trying to make sure that every word counts, and nurturing a budding idea through its page-length life is fun. For me, it's a source of flow. A while back, I was leaning toward shutting down the book-editing end of my business, but in reflecting on how that work can put me in flow, I'm leaning back. I'm editing a science-fiction novel right now, and it's good fun.

Look for those moments in your work that also feel like play, where both your mind and your mouth might be humming, where Poirot's "little grey cells" are singing in chorus. That's the work you'll do best, and the best work you'll do.

But man, the next contest I enter, I'm going to get the details straight.

Web Distractions (Or, Watching Dancing Cats Does Not a Writer Make)

Time to discuss how the Internet is both the bane and the boon to writing. Let's get baneful first.

Some time back, I had a writing project open on my screen, while looking at a Twitter stream, and also listening (well, my ears took in noise) to a webinar, which was going to end on the hour, and be followed by another webinar. Oh, the humanity! Now the webinar material wasn't just mindless prattle; it was sound information on building a bigger blogging audience, and the one that followed also offered insightful information on revising a novel. And I'd seen some great tweeted links to intriguing topical news and the amusing oddments of humanity in the tweeted flow.

But the whole of it, the tapestry of electronic screeching tires, colored balloons, half-cooked flotsam—I sensed that the inner nutrient levels were low. Trying to look more than two tweets ahead, I know this is unsustainable behavior, on a spiritual as well as logical level.

But just to add to the feeling of this cascade described above—the "is that a mouse running up my leg before I'm going to make an important speech while someone in the audience is having electroshock administered"—while I was webinaring and tweeting and reading and wobbling, I opened this post[46] from Jonathan Fields, which prompted me to record this whole scenario in the first place. There, he squints at this collected

[46] http://www.jonathanfields.com/blog/invest-in-emerging-humanity/

connectivity, and the accompanying potential of disconnect that can come from it.

The Sunday Picnic Basket of the Web

The Net indeed can seem like the largest Sunday picnic basket of all, with juicy treats shared among smiling friends and extended family, and perhaps I'm biting the keyboard that feeds me by saying "no mas, no mas," but sheesh, I'm concerned that I'm turning into one of those mice that hits the lever to drop the cocaine, and the lever taps are happening more frequently.

There have been a few published studies that suggest (as Fields alludes to) that our heavy use of the Internet and its popcornings of *this* and *now this*, but *this too!* is reshaping our abilities to have deep, concentrated focus on a subject—indeed attenuating our abilities to focus at all.

One thing I'm doing more of (with a nod to Leo Babauta)[47] is to try and close out my full desktop of overlapping applications and just have a single naked document onscreen, so that it gets full attention. Thus I'm less tempted to jump to the browser to search for pancake recipes or to my email to see if the pope has written back. Some people use the most bare bones of word processors, without any palettes or menus showing, in order to crystalize focus, but I'm not distracted by menus. Except in restaurants.

I had a nice device called a Neo a ways back, which was a dedicated word processor of sorts. Neos have a built-in keyboard,

[47] http://zenhabits.net/

boot up in a heartbeat, run forever on rechargeable batteries, and could also be used to hammer in loose nails on the deck. I wish I still had it for taking on trips, for those times when a full computer is overkill, but I sold it a while back to buy additions to my twig collection, or something like that. But long before that, I had a magnificent Underwood typewriter, which required brisk workouts with free weights to pound the keys, and which would have produced a seismic reading of 6.5 if dropped out of a plane. Those were the days.

Computer Narcosis, Internet Brain and Gosh, Where Did the Time Go?

As I commented on the Fields piece, I also fear potential neurological re-shapings, that perhaps will suppress the ability to absorb in any reflective way long-form information, in favor of the slot-machine, bells-lit flavor-packs of brain candy we can access all day long now.

Undoubtedly some brains are more susceptible to this than others. Since I've peppered mine with enough bourbon so it has more divots than most public golf courses, I might have to be more wary than most. (And our World of Warcraft recruits might be lost already, but we'll need them to man the expanding air force of drones that will soon be used to both kill terrorists and to perhaps shoot the fingers off of people texting while driving.)

Me, after musing on the Fields post (at the very moment I was being buffeted by the cluster bombs of divided electronic attentions), I vowed to no longer do these data-crams. It might be the bourbon that's trenched my memory, but it feels like I'm getting so little retained value anyway from all the podcasts, webinars, PDFs and tweets that concurrently flood my bloodshot eyeballs.

When I ask, does all this stuff, despite its twinkly appeal, make me any happier? Smarter? Better?

No.

The Net and its wonders have been an immeasurable boon to my work, but that horrible sucking sound of my soul draining away has to be listened to as well. Of course I'm still going to be there typing away, but not while opening the curtains on all sides to every passing circus. One thing at a time. Breathe. Balance. (And maybe just a bit more coffee.)

Since I made that vow, I have honored it. Except for the times I haven't. But I've been better. (You can tweet that, but don't tweet me to look at it.)

Venturing a Trembling Foot Forward into Internet Insanity

Hope I'm not piling on, but I want to continue exploring the electronic wasteland a bit more, with more pundits punditsizing.

I read with interest (and fear and loathing) a review of Nick Carr's *The Shallows: What the Internet Is Doing to Your Brain* book. I'll do here exactly what Mr. Carr treats as one of the disquieting subjects of his work: I'll distill his book in a few sentences. In essence, he posits that the always-on, ever-spilling-over information font of the Internet is actually changing the nature of our brains. His position is that this *next-next-next* ad infinitum serving of info appetizers is resulting in an attenuation of the contemplative process, a wall to the deeper mulling over subject or sphere (and being able to distinguish which is important and which is simply "now"), and potentially in the loss of our ability to reflect at a sustained level.

That made me consider how much advice on presenting information on the Net, particularly for copywriters, emphatically states that you must "chunk" information: render it in small, easily digestible paragraphs, preferably those not burdened with compound or complex sentences. Before anyone protests, of course I recognize that making any parallel between a broad—even philosophical—reading of how we now apprehend the world and how copywriters (with their loathsome goals of extolling benefits and persuading buyers) work their words might seem strained.

Fast-Food Information

But it's a personal issue for me, because I am both a marketing copywriter and a fiction writer, and though I can readily compartmentalize the two, they still share an information DNA: communicating, spreading ideas, making sparks in the head. If Mr. Carr is right (and I've only read the review, not the book, so I'm stretching here), the Netheads of this world, a world that's ever-expanding, will no longer have the hunger for—or even the skill to fully interpret—deep, thoughtful works.

For some reason, reading the Carr piece made me think of *Crime and Punishment,* how the central character, Raskolnikov (mentioned in my Johnny Cash piece earlier), frets, fusses and agonizes over the killing of the pawnbroker, and later, has his psyche roil while undergoing the ferret-like questioning of the investigator Porfiry. Raskolnikov's unease skirts near madness, and it's a cumulative state, a long building of narrative tension and revelation.

Would today's readers just want the Cliff Notes: "Poor student goes crazy after killing pawnbroker and goes to prison to rot"? That chunking summary is a dry cracker in the mouth of a sensuous, wine-mad, multi-course meal of a novel, a thousand spices and ten-story conversations.

Years back, there was a fabulous article in the New York Times titled "Tuna's End,"[48] an elegiac piece about the survival potentials (dubious) of the "wild ocean" and that of some of its top-of-the-chain denizens (here, bluefin tuna) though our depredations. It's a nicely written and sharply compelling piece, but quite long. I remember myself skimming, looking for the high points. And going back and forth to my email and the project I was working on in between the skimmings. Even being aware that I was giving short shrift to the article didn't stop me from being pulled in multiple directions.

This is your brain on chunking.

We Did Survive Elvis

I worry that Carr's right, that our scanning for immediacy, our appetites stimulated to hunger for the new, will result in an ever-

---

[48] http://www.nytimes.com/2010/06/27/magazine/27Tuna-t.html

more shallow analysis that is self-reinforcing. I worry about distinguishing the important from the trivial, if I can only absorb either in chunks.

But then I think I'm carrying the same hoary "The End Is Nigh" sign that my parents carried because of Elvis in the 50s, and that their parents carried because of jitterbugging in the 30s and that Fred and Wilma Flintstone carried because the latest stone wheels had sidewalls.

Ahh, well. I hope richer thought will survive, amidst the ephemera. I was heartened to read Molly Ringle's grand prizewinning entry for the Bulwer-Lytton Fiction Contest, awarded for the composition of the opening sentence to the worst of all possible novels:

"For the first month of Ricardo and Felicity's affair, they greeted one another at every stolen rendezvous with a kiss — a lengthy ravenous kiss, Ricardo lapping and sucking at Felicity's mouth as if she were a giant cage-mounted water bottle and he were the world's gerbil."

Molly doesn't believe in that chunking stuff; had she sallied forth and written the full novel, I'd judge it would be 1,456 pages of delicious prose. Heck, Raskolnikov might have even made it in there too.

PS I know you skimmed all of the above material, but I forgive you. I did too.

Strangled Tweets and Tortured Texts

Let's press on by reviewing some declarations about Twitter and the wholesale destruction of the universe by checking out a post by Leo Bottary, who was riffing on a *Wired* article citing a five-year study[49] of student writing conducted at Stanford University by Dr. Andrea Lunsford.

Here's what Mr. Bottary wrote:

"I hear people lament the demise of the English language all the time. They speak to how texting, tweeting, and other such practices are contributing to poor grammar, marginal spelling, and an inability to express oneself 'properly' in the written form. Lunsford disagrees. She claims, 'I think we're in the midst of a literacy revolution the likes of which we haven't seen since Greek civilization.' And as Thompson points out, 'For Lunsford, technology isn't killing our ability to write. It's reviving it—and pushing our literacy in bold new directions.'

Among other things, Lunsford's study shows they are highly attuned to their audiences and write with a sense of purpose and persuasion that is actually at a higher level when compared with previous generations. The fact that today's young people write so frequently across so many different platforms may not make them better writers in the classic sense, but the evidence suggests they may be stronger communicators than their parents. Rather than criticizing and judging our young people, this is an area where we should learn from them."

Forgive me for quoting people quoting people that are quoting people, but I found it an intriguing topic: with more means of

[49] http://ssw.stanford.edu/

communication than ever, and ever more people exercising those means, how does that affect the quality of communication? Do Twitterers that tweet every 22 minutes hone their writing (and even thinking) ability over time, or are they just twits?

Is there even a basis—or need—to consider "quality" of communications when much of what is being discussed here is transient information? Though, as shown repeatedly, nothing is truly transient on the Web.

Snotty "Professional" Writer Weighs In

It did make me wonder if in days to come, there will some tweets that will be revered like Shakespearean sonnets and worthy of reviews, i.e.,

"140 characters of apocalyptic chill, melded with childlike sing-song innocence. Ranks with Eliot's *Wasteland* for audacity, scope and cultural indictment."
— *New York Times Review of Tweets*

I'm an old crustacean, though I do use Twitter, but I do think there's language skill-building in the rising incidence of communication outreach, whether blogging, tweeting or arranging the letters in the alphabet soup of your lunch partner.

And it's reasonable to be questioning the value of high-flown scholastic language requirements in academic settings, when the value of an assignment is based on old patterns of regurgitating leaden information in the same stilted phrasings.

There is something attractive in the vivid, short bursts of thought you see everywhere online—and there's something electric in seeing people interested in connecting through new forms.

But man, there's a lot of crap writing out there, and I don't mean just of the "U R Sweet" or hair-on-fire political polemic. I read a lot of stuff produced by people trying to persuade, but they don't have any tools of persuasion. Sure, you might be able to build a lean-to of sorts with just a hammer, but not a house. And a house with working plumbing and a view? If someone is trying to shape an argument or point of view, they need more rhetorical tools than "You suck!"

The Sentence Chiropractor

Sometimes you want a sentence to bend, sometimes you want it to snap. Some word-journeys can't be made unless you can roll the words down language hills, stall them at a cliffside, pick a metaphorical flower in the meadow and set some verbal pitons to clamber back up those hills.

I'm with other pundits in that I think your thought processes improve the more you work with the abstractions of language—its elasticity works well with your brain's plasticity. Having the tools means you can build a more complex structure—maybe even a cathedral, rather than a mere house with working plumbing.

Of course, if you want to just order a sandwich, that doesn't have to be done in iambic pentameter. But it's a shame to settle for limited expression when there's so much sex in deeper language, so many bright strawberries, so many dank, dangerous corners and beguiling fragrances.

Then again, in some situations, a good old Anglo-Saxon "Fuck that!" is sometimes the most eloquent response.

If a Question Falls in the Forest ...

Of course, maybe there isn't even a question to answer here. To go musical metaphor on you, from every Elvis Presley hip-waggling that presaged the decline of civilization to the Stones to the Sex Pistols to Nirvana to Marilyn Manson to Lady Gaga, there have been people outraged and startled by the new. There is movement and jostling and crudity amid new styles of expression, but there is still much quality writing about, whether 300-word blog post or David Foster Wallace's 1088-page *Infinite Jest.*

I must confess, though, I do believe in the thrill, drama and risk of skillful punctuation (be still, my beating apostrophe!) *and* pungent writing, now and forever, one and inseparable.

[*Note to prospective copywriting clients: I will never include any "Fuck thats" in content I provide, unless by request. A well-placed "Dear Me!" can sometimes convey the essence.*]

Trying to (Not) Lend Distraction an Ear

Everybody's getting hammered with distractions these days. The sweet candy of the smartphone turns into a shrill mistress clamoring for attention. The bright chirps of the Twitter feed turn into an ear-splitting cacophony, ever *pecking, pecking, pecking.* Trying to keep up with your grandma's blog makes it hard to read every post from Buzzfeed too.

Writers, how can you find your sweet solace at the keyboard, where the only music you hear are the words in tune, when all around you are the beeps, buzzes and bombs of our 25/7 (extra credit) world?

Well, beats me. I'm a lousy example. But now I'm going to huff and puff and declare that (after many such declarations), I'm really—no, really—going to create new habits of discipline and focus. Because, dangit, how am I ever going to get any writing done? Here are my main problems, with a few solutions:

News, Not Needed

I always wanted to be a journalist. Perhaps with newspapers fluttering their way into time's crypt, it's just as well I never got an actual job on a paper. But I jones to read the news, even if it's mostly fervid enumerations of political atrocities or social atrocities (newest Kardashian cut, anyone?). Thus I'll read news updates throughout the day. Not gonna do that anymore. From now, just a morning look at the headlines, and maybe a glance or two at the excellent Next Draft[50] news curation after lunch. No more swallowing the vortex of human misery—just enough to get bloody.

---

[50] http://nextdraft.com/

Bigger Data to Fry

As I blathered on about earlier, I write marketing copy for businesses. So I try to keep up on all kinds of developments in marketing info, like marketing automation programs, lead generation, effective landing pages, big data, big bad data and big, bad badass data. Attend all kinds of webinars and the like, to see the breadth of marketing concerns. No more. No more webinars and articles that don't have direct relevance to the kind of copy I write. Maybe just check in with the good MarketingProfs[51] daily newsletter, and cherry-pick the articles of relevance.

Eating Fewer Essays

I love long-form writing, the kind of stuff you see on Medium and Longreads and in the *New Yorker* and the *Atlantic*. I'm an essay writer myself, and there are some excellent prose stylists around these days to really show you (me) how it's done. But get into a few of those pieces, and you're an hour or more down (and your own essay lies a'dying). Can't do that anymore—one long-form essay, if any, per day. Or read them after the workday is done. Yeah, I can spare some time from the television, another scouring desert wind of the mind.

The Creaks, Shakes and Conniptions of Publishing

I'm fascinated by the publishing industry, the creaks and shakes and conniptions it's undergone in the last five years or so, since readers and self-publishing (and hybrid publishing, and agent-

[51] http://www.marketingprofs.com/

assisted publishing and cooperative publishing and every other garden-seedling variant) came into ascendancy. But I've spent so many hours reading about the end of print, the bloody cudgel named Amazon, the imperative that every writer have a bouncy, groomed platform or they will shrivel and die—nay! Nevermore. Perhaps I'll just periodically check in with an industry maven who pokes into every corner, like the silver-tongued, indefatigable Porter Anderson,[52] who adjudicates publishing boxing matches at joints like Thought Catalog and Publishing Perspectives.

A Deaf Ear to the Mail Bell

And email, damn. I check email 20 times a day, another one of those mouse-pressing-the-cocaine-lever things. There's no need. It just breaks your focus, so that if you did, by Odin's beard, happen to be engaged in a piece of writing, it takes fifteen minutes to return to that fugue state of concentration that good writing deserves. Not gonna do it anymore: email in the morning, after lunch and at the end of the day.

By the way, Ed Gandia consistently offers good counsel about focus and productivity, as does John Soares. Google 'em and check 'em out. And here's a fine series of pieces[53] on the myth of multitasking, and how to mind (and effectively mine) your own mind by Therese Walsh at the great Writer Unboxed site.

Despite me not reading every headline, or offering all my ears

---

[52] http://porteranderson.com/about/

[53] http://writerunboxed.com/2015/04/14/no-time-to-write-maximize-your-minutes-multitasking-series-part-3/

at every webinar, the world will go on. I really won't miss out. And I'll get more writing done. Your writing distractions might differ from mine, but it can only be good for your own writing to consider how to cut them back.

Oh, yeah: don't stop reading my stuff, though. You can return to your own writing anytime.

And Speaking of Extraordinary Wastes of Time

Speaking of writing distractions, here's a fine one: being jealous of another writer's success. I don't suggest this merely in theory (he says, as he clenches his fists, sweats and swears about another undeserving writer being touted as the next big thing, when the he himself feels like merely a thing).

If you've read into the book this far, you might have noticed that I can be a wise guy on my topics, throwing in a joke here and jibe there. But the joke for the jealous writer is really on them. Since I can speak for pretty much every one of the 143,345,981 writers in the world, trust me—it can be a problem.

It All Started in Catholic School

For me, I think the problem started in Catholic school. (When in doubt, blame the nuns.) You see, they had us learning the 10 Commandments in first or second grade, glazed-eyed reciting by gathered tykes on an almost daily basis. Consider: If you were a seven-year-old, and you were told not to covet your neighbor's wife, what would you think? I hadn't even known if I had any talent at this coveting thing, and now I was being told not to do it.

I immediately went back home and checked out the local wives to see if they were up to some covert coveting. But I wasn't so busy with that that I couldn't covet my neighbor's house as well. Covet, covet, covet.

I am only an amateur psychologist (though I will accept money for my analyses), but I got the sense that my Catholic brethren were priming the pump for us on the sin thing. You know, telling us what not to do, so its fascination impelled us into that forbidden, coveted quest. But back then, I had the mercy of confession to hose off my juvenile sins. However, since I am a lapsed Catholic, I suppose this shriven screed is my confession.

Pathetic Timewasters and Other Jolly Pursuits

This I know: being jealous of your fellow writers' triumphs is a mighty pathetic waste of time. As Carrie Fisher said, "Resentment is like drinking poison and waiting for the other person to die." Too often I've squirmed and twitched when

I've read about the incredible contracts given to contemporary authors, soaring sales figures, critical acclaim, while I'm still grubbing about trying to get an agent to spend 15 minutes with my manuscript. It's not that I want successful writers to die; perhaps just contract gangrene.

Still working on that.

So I *am* working on it. It's among my New Year's resolutions. It might sound like pabulum, but I am going to remind myself to congratulate those who do well, and to try and work all the harder on my own writing. So somebody can be jealous of me.

No, I don't mean that. Well, not all that much.

Is it OK if I still covet my neighbor's iPad Air, though?

Rejections and Scrotums (It's Not What You Think)

I want to end this section with a couple of thoughts on writing rejections. And scrotums. Trying to place an article about a man who drives nails into his scrotum is a challenge. You have to find a publication that is appropriately (or inappropriately) edgy, but as a writer with an interest in circulating ideas, not so obscure as to not have an audience. And also as a writer interested in circulating cash, you would want compensation, even for a piece that might need to have dark curtains pulled over its stage.

These concerns came to mind the other day when I received a rejection notice for my memoir-style article about a night in San Francisco many, many years ago. I'd attended what I thought was going to be a tattooing display and discussion, but its main event was an S&M demo, where aside from the scrotal crucifixion mentioned above, the artist in question sewed up his testicles over his penis with dental floss, much like a woeful pig in a blanket. Live, naked, onstage, much to my appalled eyes.

The Taste of Rejection

Where I'm going with this is not into any discussion of better choices among an evening's entertainment (my article does that), but rather the various flavors of writer's rejections, and how those taste on a writer's tongue. My rejection folder, in all its glory is two inches high, and weighs almost two pounds. You might think that by my keeping that folder, I have a different—but just as pointed—sense of masochism as my pal with the pliant scrotum. By no means.

That pile of "nos" is just a thing writers can step on to be a bit higher on their way to "yes."

Looking over my hummock of rejections, you can see traces of their evolution over time. Sure, most of them are form letters of the "Dear Author, because of the number of submissions we receive, we regret that we are unable to respond personally ..." variety. But from those publications of twenty years ago where the editorial assistants or (victory!) the editors themselves spent some effort to tell the writer just why something didn't fit the publication, the "no, buts" are longer and more developed extenuations. In the main, the handwritten rejections from the last few years are brief and pointed. They reflect more of today's hurried and "next!" pace.

In fact, the letters themselves—if you get an actual letter—these days are so much more often little strips of paper, a slight ribbon that perhaps rejects a little more softly, because the "we regret" isn't followed by the full page's damning white space of emptiness. And as the evolution of electronic publishing is pushing paper aside, physical rejection letters are fewer seen. The ease of an electronic "no" is hastening their demise. Speaking of demise, I hadn't gone through my reject slips for years, but in doing so, saw that many of the magazines I'd tried so fervidly to enter have shut their doors for good. Little solace, that.

Aiming High Keeps Your Head Up

But it was fun to flip through my collection, and note my ambition. There's a partially handwritten, partially printed (from a dot-matrix printer, oh my!) sheet from 1988 on what I pushed that year: Articles to *Atlantic, Esquire, Paris Review, Harper's, Playboy* and a host of smaller publications. None of those titans bit into what I was serving, but there was consolation in getting "an intriguing idea" from a *Harper's* editorial assistant, and a "It's a good one" from *Esquire.* A long handwritten response from a *Travel and Leisure* managing editor in 1992 detailing alternate publications that might accept my piece that he graciously declined.

Even the form salutation from the *Utne Reader:* "Dear intrepid writer:"

So many of the letters are undated and don't specifically mention the rejected article or story, so I have no idea what these limbo letters refer to, just a vagabond "no" telling me at some point I mailed, I waited, I hoped, and it was for naught. But clasping hands with those closed hands in my "no" pile are a number of yesses—the extended correspondence I had with Peter Sussman, a *San Francisco Chronicle* editor, much of it handwritten, about an article of mine[54] he published about my extended (and crazy) correspondence with the Jack Daniel's Distillery, which I mentioned in the Introduction.

A series of letters from Lynn Ferrin, the late editor of *Motorland* magazine (precursor to *Via*) who had been trying to locate

---

[54] http://www.tombentley.com/JackDanielsChronicle.pdf

me—pre-email address—in the midst of a couple of moves. Regarding my pre-Starbucks piece on driving cross-country trying to locate a good cup of coffee,[55] she told me, "Out of the piles of unreadable pap that come over the transom every day, by dump truck, suddenly there's something that stirs my coffee ..."

Onward!

Here's my deep message: keep sending your stuff out. I've had articles accepted for publication that were years old, that were sent out 10 times. My rejection folder weighs two pounds, but that's considerably less than the weight of the hundreds of magazines, newspapers or books that accepted and published pieces of mine. The reject folder is just a reminder that you have to do the work, and keep doing it. I'll pass on the advice of Howard Junker, the longtime, former editor of *ZYZZYVA* magazine, whose typed signature in his rejection letter is preceded by, "Keep the faith." And whose handwritten note reads: "Onward!"

Onward indeed. Now, can you tell me what editor is likely to go for that scrotum piece?

---

[55] http://www.tombentley.com/BadBeanFunk.pdf

7

Practical Matters/Resources

This last section of the book is going to deal with some practical writing matters. But not the kind of thing like how to prepare for your taxes, use a virtual assistant for things like transcribing interviews, or how to set prices on your work, if you're a copywriter. That kind of info can be dug up (without digging too deeply) on the Internet.

[Note: Speaking of the Internet, I do have a lot of sites mentioned here. To this point, I've been putting some URLs in the endnotes, but there are just too many here in the Resources section, so just Google them by name, and you're good to go.]

Because we're such good pals now, I want to continue in a personal vein on the practical matters that I want to write about, such as how to work with editors, how to write queries, advice on entering writing contests and entering into writing collaborations. And then round it out with a discussion of various writing tools, and cap it off with good references for both copywriters and fiction writers.

Sound good? Since I'm thinking positively today, I see you nod your head in agreement. First off, let's look at working with editors. I'm going to talk about working with editors of nonfiction magazines here, but many of the observations apply to working with editors of every stripe.

Problem Editors and Positive Editors

I know, I know, all of those editors who have rejected your queries or articles are obvious emissaries of Baal, troglodytes, fresh steaming cat poop or much worse. Over the submission years, I have declared them among the seven princes of Hell (or at least in the league of incompetent cable installers). But I recant my earlier denunciations, and with good reason.

For all of the queries flatly unanswered, or for those receiving the peremptory "We can't use this," there are editors who take the calculated moment from the lunacy of today's publishing world and offer a statement of encouragement to the anxious author. Or better yet, a response that leads said author to explore another editorial opportunity with the publication, if the initial submission doesn't cut it.

Here's an example, using two magazine editors who both exhibit those alarming traits of decency. As I've mentioned, I've written for *Airstream Life* magazine for 10 years. The editor, Rich Luhr, originally solicited me to write for his then-new magazine after he'd seen an Airstream piece of mine on the Net. Now, having an editor ask you for a piece out of the blue is gift enough, but over time Rich has grown to know my work, and often assigns a piece that's tuned to my sensibilities. Props to the man.

A while back, he was working on a new specialty magazine for Mercedes owners. I put in some time on a few articles, but Rich couldn't find the advertising base to support the publication. He had the grace to offer me a kill fee above the price I'd requested, because he knew I'd done a lot of research time. Above and beyond.

Do the Article Two-Step

That ties in well with an editor I had been corresponding with. She runs a Mercedes magazine in the UK, and I sent her one of the articles written for the lost US mag. We went back and forth a bit, and finally she decided that it wasn't right for her. But I mentioned VERY casually at the end of my "thanks for listening" that I could write a piece about my then chariot, an aged-but-stalwart 1981 SL 380.

Bingo! I have an assignment that I initially hadn't conceived of, just because an editor took the time to explore the potential of other article ideas—or because they simply opened a conversation. There are a few lessons here, but the main ones are that once you are actually having a conversation with an editor, *be conversant:* recognize that they are open to you as a writer, even if they're not immediately buying what you're writing.

And once the conversational door is open, you can walk in so much more freely than if you are sending out your first (and oftentimes) stiff query. I had a series of email exchanges with the editor of an in-flight magazine. She didn't go for my initial query, but took the time (in just a few sentences) to go over what the magazine was looking for. I sent her another query, which was discussed, and which prompted another. Now, none of these ideas actually worked for the magazine, but I know from the quality of our exchanges that I can approach this editor on a comfortable, conversant basis in the future.

I've written for the national magazine, *The American Scholar*, for almost four years. I reached the point where I could casually frame a story idea without much fuss and send it to Allen Freeman, my former editor there, who'd consider it without much fuss. By that I mean, he already knew what kind of writing I could do, so I might get a line or two about slant or about expanding/restricting the idea, or I might get something as succinct as "go for it."

There is a new section editor there, and it took me a number of queries to get back on board with what the magazine wants. But I did, which speaks to the power of persistence. Now I hope to be in the same good graces with her as I was with Allen.

We writers all like editors who tell us to go for it. Especially when they raise their per-word rates now and then, as both the *Airstream Life* and *American Scholar* editors have. Maybe they will lend me their cars.

Second Dates

And if you've published even *one* piece for a magazine, think to approach those editors again, if you have a quality idea. I have written pieces for a couple of editors who publish wine-and-spirits world magazines, and now I don't have to write a formal query with my publishing credits and other tedium; I can start right in with "Hi Tim. I had an idea for a piece ..."

Obviously, you don't want to badger editors with lame queries so that they wonder why they ever published you in the first place, but once you have an editor's ear, you're miles ahead of the game. (If you try to get their other ear, though, they might press charges.)

Don't Bollix Your Queries

Speaking of magazine editors compels me to speak of query letters, since a good example of the latter can invoke an editor to make merry with you. A bad example can invoke an editor to a brisk "No thanks." Or just "No." Or just nothing, no reply at all. Let's start out with an example of a bad (no, execrable actually) query letter sent to an agent for a fiction project.

I made this one up, but having seen some examples from editors of queries they'd received, my parody is not far from the pieces that prompt editorial screams.

The bit of bilge I penned below shows you how to oppress and alienate a literary agent with your fiction project. (Note: if you steal my sterling idea about the novel, I demand the foreign-film rights.) Below that is an actual query for an article of mine that was published in Writer's Digest[56] long years back. Note that the first few lines of my real query's lead are the published article's

[56] http://www.tombentley.com/CraftingEssay.pdf

lead as well: write the query lead as though it could be the article lead—it displays your writing chops, organizes your thinking about the rest of the article, and it will save you time as well.

The So Bad, It's Good (and Ugly)

Dear Agent (If you aren't the right agent for my pitch, please forward this to the right agent. And please let me know you've forwarded it, and to who. I mean "whom." Whomever it was forwarded to, that is. Whatever.):

So, I'm pretty sure I've invented a new, popular genre for my 263,437-word novel, The Nightmare from Which I Never Woke: I call it "high-fi, transmedia sci-fi." It's high-fi because I wrote the whole thing during a series of peyote-induced trances. In the desert. So, it's like pure and all.

It's transmedia because it will have some clickable pages that will send the reader to websites where they can order t-shirts. It's sci-fi because the world I created has two suns. (I can work with editors if they need it to be three.)

Anywho, there's some saga-like multigenerational stuff on my main planet, Hortog, and wars with lots of futuristic weapons (with step-by-step details on their manufacture and operations). But it's really a love story, because my main character, Glig, has sex with an alien, who's kind of like an old-fashioned eggbeater.

The novel's also very meta. You know, self-referential and informing.

My mother has been hounding me to send this query, because I haven't had much income for a bit, so if you could send me a little chunk of the advance now, that might help get her off my back. By the way, I paid for one of those deep Internet searches to find out your home address, so if you'd like to discuss this in person, I'm there in a heartbeat. I know you are busy—I will bring the coffee!

By the way, if you aren't interested in this book, I also write a kind of YA-haiku combination that is killer.

PS I think my novel could be a series.

No-Nos

This query stinks up the joint because it addresses a generic agent (agents love the names their mothers gave them), it ruminates on pointless issues, it's specific when it should be general, it's general when it should be specific, and in offering to stalk the editor at a coffee klatch, it veers into prosecutable grounds. Though that YA-haiku thing might work, if it had a banging DJ.

The Good (Even My Mother Thinks So)

Dear Maria Schneider:

First-person essays span space, time and subject: the city dump, an obsessive bird, or a toy from the 60s—all subjects of essays I've published—are just one shuffle of an endless deck of compelling themes. It's never the subject of an essay that tells, but the style and stance of its author. What might seem the least likely of essay subjects can be made a piquant page-turner by a writer's winning hand.

I propose an article for Writer's Digest on Crafting the Personal Essay.

The article would cover these sections:

Topics

- *How to choose a subject that suits your style (and vice versa)*
- *Finding subjects in everyday life*

- *Fleshing out topics (whether they are existing personal interests or burgeoning ones)*

Slant

- *Distinction between slant and topic*
- *How to choose, apply and maintain essay tone*
- *How to blend personal perspective with facts*

Voice

- *The presence of the author (formal/informal, in the background or up front)*
- *Avoiding heavy-handedness while promoting point of view*
- *Authority with a light touch*

The Lead

- *How to hook the reader*
- *Building on the lead*
- *The use of declarative sentences, humor, restraint and exaggeration*
- *Divergence from the lead*

Rhythm

- *Structure and cadence*
- *The musicality of words*
- *How to sneak up on a reader, and how to overwhelm them*
- *Maintaining momentum and topic drive*
- *Layering of ideas*

Conclusions

- *Packing a punch at the end*
- *Circling back from your lead*

- *Customer (reader) satisfaction*

Markets

- *Pitching your story*

For relevant article sections, I'll provide short examples of good and bad expressions of the outlined technique or approach. I will also cite some examples of essay compendiums that are strong representations of first-person essay writing, such as Philip Lopate's The Art of the Personal Essay.

I've published essays or stories in the San Francisco Chronicle, Traveler's Tales, the San Jose Mercury News (West and SV magazines), Things magazine, Verbatim magazine, and others. My website, www.tombentley.com has a number of my published pieces under the Freelance and Fiction links.

Please reply or give me a call if you're interested in seeing my manuscript or in discussing the query further.

I look forward to hearing from you.

Regards,

Tom Bentley

Yes-Yesses

This query is directed to a specific (and relevant) editor, it opens with a strong lead, it clearly and explicitly discusses the article scope, it has some writer's bio info, and it invites the editor to discuss the article possibilities. The editor is given a good sense of what the writer could do with the potentials outlined in the query.

And b'God, they even paid decently for it.

Leading with the Right Hook (in Your Query)

Should I eat the box first?

Have you ever noticed that the way certain things are packaged or presented instantly influences your feelings about them? In this age of Malcolm Gladwell's *Blink* or the myriad of studies about marketing preferences or tastes, savvy shoppers are aware that a rice package that has an artfully designed classic "homey," or retro or "Miz Maybelle's Cajun Rice Paddy" look might contain nothing better inside than old-school Rice-a-Roni (which was never really embraced by San Francisco for its alleged treatness to begin with).

Yet, even if we know that the packaging is pointedly positioned to persuade, it's hard to be objective. The photo above shows the packaging for a pair of bath soaps, sandwiching a box of individually wrapped chocolates. Indeed, the soaps were quite nice, and the chocolates delightful, but their artful and expensive packaging immediately disposed me favorably toward them, psychically relieving me of at least a smidgen of critical objectivity.

Apple does this very well with their packaging, everything done just so, from the typography to the way the electronic components rest snugly in their recessed cubbies. The "Tiles" box above is indicative: these weren't mere chocolate squares, but "tiles." This told you they were special little chocolates, with a bit of architectural snootiness. The packaging, of course, tells a story. Check out this link for an interesting take[57] from Seth Godin on putting a worldview in your packaging.

---

[57] http://sethgodin.typepad.com/seths_blog/2010/02/the-brand-the-package-the-story-and-the-worldview.html

And WTF Does This Have to Do with Writing?

Glad you asked. One of the chunky nuggets of advice you'll get about sending a query to a magazine editor is that you lead your query with your article lead, like what I did in the query above. Write the actual first paragraph of the article you intend to write and that's what your editor-in-waiting looks at when they open your cleverly crafted email. Your product's packaging is immediately in their face, so that they know your article is "Dreadnought Dave's Eye-Searing Hot Sauce" or "Winsome Winnie's Willow Bark Soap." They can taste your writing immediately, not having to wade through "Dear Editor Toadstool: I'd like to write a piece for Amalgamated Amalgams on surfactants that subside, and rarely surface. I'd cover these fascinating points..."

Here's a query lead I used about a proposed article on bathtub distilling that did grab an editor and that indeed did begin the published article itself:

Maybe it's the down economy, maybe it's a renewal of that do-it-yourself ethic that characterizes this country, or maybe it's because it's a closed-door, wink-wink, just-the-other-side-of-legal enterprise, but there's a resurgence of home and hobby spirits distillers. Your neighbor might not make home-brewed hooch, but there's a fair chance he knows how to get a hold of a bottle or two.

This "in media res" style of querying has worked for me a number of times. However, I spent some time shopping an article on roller derby gals for which the query begins thusly:

What's got a raucous crowd, a heart-pounding pace requiring strength, stamina and mad skills, an undertone of potential violence, a flash of spandexed sexuality and enough tattoos to open a carney parlor? Why, roller derby, of course—and Santa Cruz, California roller derby in particular. Roller derby has speed-skated its way to tremendous popularity in the US over the past decade, returning from what was represented as a sort of underclass—though popular—theatrical spectacle in the 50s and 60s. There are leagues all over the country, and national organizations such as the Women's Fast Track Derby Association, which counts nearly 100 leagues under its skates.

Disclaimer: All You Editors Out There About to Receive Queries: I Don't Mean You

That paragraph above is how I wanted to start the actual article, because I think it's vivid, particular and expressive. But, I sent that query out to 12 separate relevant publications, and only received a single reply. (The fact that many magazines or papers often don't even send out a polite—or even impolite—"no" these days should be the topic of another section.) Though I do like the feeling of the query lead, and think it tells an editor what the article would feel like, perhaps something is lacking. Or perhaps it simply doesn't fit the editor's calendar, the magazine's style, or any of a number of reasons, quality of expression notwithstanding, for which a piece doesn't flutter the hearts (assuming editors have them) of your magazinish recipients.

I have a small collection of liquor flasks, most of which are very nice pieces of metal tooling. Many of them are quite old, with beautiful engraving or filigree, delightful in their heavy feeling in the hand. But I have a couple that also look quite nice, but there's something off: the base metal is cheaper and lighter, the metalwork not finished with flair or with that quiet competence that indicates quality. So maybe there's something cheesy about the roller derby lead I'm not seeing.

Keep sending those queries out and keep tailoring their packaging with your writer's eye.

For some great examples of successful queries, get the free downloads (and sign up for the great newsletters) from Linda Formichelli at The Renegade Writer and Mridu Khullar Relph at The International Freelancer.

Round Out Your Thoughts: Write in an Airstream

Let's move from queries to silvery roundnesses.

Can your writing environment be a factor in your writing? The answer's obvious, if say, you were trying to write romantic sonnets, while two feet from your hair-raised head a teeth-bared pit bull strained against a cracking leash. That's a bit extreme of course. But might you write halfway better if half of the pit bull's teeth were removed? How would a purring kitten in the room affect your writing?

I broach the topic because I write in somewhat of an unusual environment: attacked by plaid. That's my 1966 Airstream Globetrotter in the photo above. It's got a good broadband connection (though it's only sends Internet packets from the 60s, so there's a lot of "The Man from Uncle" coming through) and it's downright cozy.

As I've mentioned, I live in a semi-rural environment, so out of its many windows I see mostly fields, right now filled with high grasses—and the skunk I missed stepping on by two feet the other day.

You already know I write regularly for *Airstream Life* magazine; I've written a lot about the feeling of being in an old Airstream. So, to quote myself:

The Airstream's classic silvery-egg shapeliness has been refined, modified and expanded over time, but that bullet-bodied essence has retained its original appeal. There are certain shapes that beguile the eye, winning our affections in a swift, unconscious bond that escapes any internal editor. Perhaps more intimately, there's something a little womb-like about the trailers; they curl around you when you're relaxing inside. That singular shape still rewards the eye with a tingle of approval; every glance reinforces the sense of timeless design.

I do feel that congenial cocooning in the old trailer, and I think it's a fine environment for writing: there's the sound of the mockingbirds (and sometimes those damn roosters), the wind swaying the shifting grasses, and that settled sense of an old vehicle that's still solid and sound. I think well in the old Stream, and it feels like an atmosphere conducive to good keyboarding.

But some writers do well with an entirely different ambience. I know writers who love to go to active coffee shops for their scribblings, needing the murmurs of people and the spoosh of the espresso machine to percolate their thoughts. Other people make sure there ARE no windows in their writing room, so distraction can't seep in. I'm one of those people who never writes with music playing, or at least music with lyrics, because I'm lured by the words, and my writing thought train derails.

I love to write travel pieces, but don't like to write the actual sentence-by-sentence of an article on the road. So I'll write notes and a few sentences in the hotel room, but I always wait to get back home to put together the full composition. Of course, I do some of my writing in the house too, because that's where the bourbon is.

I return to my Airstream when I want a room of my own. Where do you hang your writing hat?

Winning Ain't Everything, But ...

Now let's go from silver bullets to silver (and maybe even gold) medals. It's great to get published. I've had the good fortune to be published in lots of magazines and newspapers, and as I alluded to earlier, I'm grateful for the editors who have given me the opportunity, particularly when I first started out, and had nary a clip to my name. But there's a special—and sometimes odd—kick that comes from doing well in a writing contest.

There's some ego investment there for sure. But I think the ego vector comes less from, "Wow, did I kick Shakespeare's old booty all over the place in that haiku contest!" than Sally Field's famous, " ... this time I feel it—and I can't deny the fact that you like me, right now, you like me!"

Writers can be inward sorts, languishing a league or two below the surface in their writing caves, so validation of any sort is manna precious.

The reason I bring up writing contests right now is that a bit back I won third place in a travel-writing contest over at Dave's Travel Corner online. It's the second contest in which I've ridden in the winner's circle over at Dave's—I won second place in the year before's contest.

Dave had solicited contest prizes from some of his travel industry connections; tallying the swag for both contests comes to $200 cash, four travel books, a travel wallet, a certificate for a private tasting for six ($180 value) at a fancy-schmancy Napa winery, a travel backpack, a Vegas.com promotional kit (one article is set in Vegas) that included a deck of cards, nice poker chips, coasters and more, and last but not least chewy: two big packs of licorice vines. Now them's some winnin's.

Paying to Play

Dave had the generous spirit not to charge for entry into his contest, but many contests do require entry fees. I've seen novel writing contests where the fees went upward of $125, but of course, reviewing novels for contest entries could take up a great deal of reading time. Many contests I've entered were free, but a good number of them required entry fees between $10 and $25. Some years I've spent $100 for contests, others maybe half that much. But I've had fair luck.[58]

Two years back, I enjoyed a free year of Carol Tice's Freelance Writing Den[59] (normally $25 a month), and found the Den a deep well of excellent writing resources, as well as a congenial place for writers to congregate. I won that free year just by writing—no fee—a blog post. Here's my doffed cap to Carol and the aforementioned Linda Formichelli for choosing me.

I've won tickets to a Broadway play; admission, lodging and meals at a good writer's conference; a few cash prizes of $100 or more, and long ago, that lovely glass plaque that adorns this section. Being named on anything with John Steinbeck's name is good gravy. And it came with $1,000 cash and that Leon Panetta presented it to me (in lieu of an ill Thomas Steinbeck, John's son), making that gravy all the warmer.

---

[58] http://www.tombentley.com/tom-bentley-writing-contests-and-awards/

[59] http://freelancewritersden.com/

My most recent contest winner has a tinge of sadness to it, because the subject of the piece was my first-true love, who disappeared on a Columbian river many years ago, a story I'd linked earlier. I'd heard about the Past Loves story contest, and my piece was poignant enough to come away with the $100 first prize.

Contests (With Caveats), Si!

Contests can give you good exposure. They can also stretch your writing: you will often be given a theme or a prompt to follow, and it can be a helpful challenge to push your words into places they wouldn't go otherwise. And sometimes you might be able to enter an article or a story with a piece that you'd written some time ago and hadn't found a home for. Don't forget that Sally Field thrill. Not to mention, there's the potential for licorice.

Make sure the contest is credible, make sure to follow the contest guidelines to the letter, and of course, don't spend money that you can't afford. (I've lost WAY more contests than I've won.) I was going to list a lot of writing contest resources, but the smart fellow at The Competitive Writer[60] has already done that.

He provides links to writing contest advice and resources, like Hope Clark's great Funds for Writers[61] newsletter and Moira Allen's Writing World, two newsletters I always look forward to receiving, and which contain good contest listings. [Note: Moira has since suspended her newsletter.] He also lists contest

---

[60] http://www.competitivewriter.com/

[61] http://fundsforwriters.com

databases, care of fine publications like *Poets and Writers.* One other source not on his list is the yearly *Writer's Market,* which can be obtained in print or online or both. That publication has a Contests and Awards section that lists contest specs, fees, deadlines and prizes.

Oh, but don't enter any of the ones I intend to. I'm sensitive, you know.

Get Properly Prompted

How about having a contest with yourself? You can challenge your writing mind in unusual ways by feeding it some writing prompts. Writing prompts are small sparklers that can light up corners of your writing mind, corners that might remain dark without the nudge.

Prompts can be so completely off the wall—"Describe how your intestines would try to parallel-park a minivan"—that your conventional approach to storytelling is struck dumb: a new tongue can be induced to speak.

Writing in other voices, other colors and other textures is a way to unleash your imagination's beast. Roar!

There are a number of sites on the Net that supply good writing prompts. If a character in one of your stories goes mute, or a plot point doesn't seem to have a point, they can be a good way to get your writing threads unglued. Writing for five minutes on some fizzy subject could loosen whatever is reining you in on your bigger project.

Here are some sites:

StoryWonk
Creative Writing Prompts
Writer's Digest Prompts
Creative Writing Solutions
One Minute Writer
On Twitter: @writingprompts

And for fun and as examples, here are a couple of my pieces I zipped off, a few minutes per. One was to put myself in the mind of a vegetable (not too hard in my case) and another in the mind of a metal. Both of them appear to have some self-esteem problems.

It's Not Easy Being Green

"Uhh, something's not right," the bell pepper said aloud. I feel something damp right at my feet, she thought. No, not quite damp, no, more like mossy, yes mossy.

She strained to see her tiny feet, but being a bell pepper, could do nothing more than glimpse a bit of the soft green swell of her belly. It's itchy too, she thought.

Then with an abrupt tightening of her shoulders (which being a bell pepper, didn't tighten all that much), she realized it: she was moldy! Moldy, her, and not even two weeks old. She stifled a sob, and then groaned. She sensed the nearby celery shrinking back from her.

Iron's Bluff Is Called

Nothing's nobler than Iron, Iron Eddy thought. All those other pre-

tenders, magnesium, sulphur, silicate—hah! Losers, pathetic wannabes. I alone am iron-hearted, iron willed. He looked quickly around and then said under his breath, "But I've been hearing some rumors, ugly rumors. It got back to me that my mother wasn't pure!"

He bestirred his tight neck and raised his voice: "Nonsense! Just look at me, red-blooded in every way!" But he cast his eyes down, to the ore of his soul, and murmured, "But what about those striations of blue. Surely no one can see their vile shadows ..."

Get Prompted, Get Productive

I know, I know, works of genius, aren't they? But fun! Check out those prompt sites and fling some sentences into the universe. They might orbit around in your head long enough to spur you on write something with more gravity.

Typing with Another Writer's Hands

I told you I was going to jump all over the place in this practical matters section, and this jump is going to take you right (write) into the arms of another writer. Better brush your teeth.

Writers I've known (myself prominently among them) often argue with themselves. Should it be *that* character whose hand is crushed in the tractor? Would a flashback scene in the second chapter be too clichéd? Is the novel best set in Provence, or perhaps Peoria? These might be dodges to procrastinate from the writing (another habit that writers execute with vigor), but it's more that there are a host of structural and textual decisions to be made in a story's unfolding, and competing claims are made in an author's mind when he or she attempts to commit to the page.

Add another writer into the mix? Clash of the Titans!

Or perhaps more accurately, clash of authorial sensibility, which is a broad cloth of past writing experience, favored author influences, writing intent/motivation—those and more, all the way down to critical compositional inclinations, like whether you are a writer that likes a verb to prance merrily away from its subject wearing flounce skirts of subordinate clause, plus taffeta layers of adverb and adjective.

Or one whose verbs are a clean shot. Bang.

Wedded to Another Writer's Work

Thus, adding another writer into that existing goulash of conscious/subconscious deliberations, false starts and bloodshot-eyed writing jags (contrasted with two weeks of writing drought) seems an invitation to a wedding that's failed before the vows are cast.

Now, I'd never collaborated, nor really considered collaboration on any fiction projects. But I was aware that Johnny Truant and Sean Platt have been writing multiple fiction-series projects together for a while, and doing quite well, both in the writing and the selling of the writing. So, a model.

A little while back I edited an epic novel for a friend, Rick

Wilson,[62] The Storytelling Dentist. (He doesn't call himself that, and deserves a much more eloquent tag that befits both his medical and writing prowess, but that's all I came up with for the moment.)

Rick's novel, which has the equally epic title of *The Man Who Wore Mismatched Socks,*[63] is a sweeping story that begins in WWII England and stretches into the 1960s. It's soaked in brio, heartfelt humanity, sacrifice, skullduggery, romance, cowardice and glory—and all that's probably just chapter one. So I'm quite familiar with Rick's style.

Out of the blue, I got this from him:

Hey Tom:
In other news, an old college friend posted a phrase on Facebook, describing a large icicle, that is quite simply a magnificent book title:

"Swirled all the way to the shrub"

I can't let it go. Here's a crazy idea: Wanna write a short story together, with that title as the jumping off point? I don't have a lot of time these days, so I'm not proposing anything at breakneck speed. Could be a hoot though.

"Swirled All the Way to the Shrub"
Rick

---

[62] http://rickwilsondmd.typepad.com

[63] http://www.amazon.com/The-Man-Wore-Mismatched-Socks/dp/0991301757/

Starting the Story's Engine

Rick, who also has a talent and penchant for vivid character names, supplied some starters, one of which seemed to scream for the page: Pinky DeVroom. We decided to try alternating chapters. Here's my opening story paragraph:

Pinky DeVroom, in his cups, stared into his brandy. His lips appeared to be having a complex argument, flexing and jutting without a clear rhythm. The argument's fulcrum was the removal of the characteristic sneer from those lips, but the pivot was coming to rest: the sneer won.

The Shrub, just to keep you from dying of suspense, became the Prohibition-era speakeasy that Pinky, a Boston society-column newspaperman frequents. The era is essential, because the story starts just short of the Crash of '29, which torques Pinky's world, along with most of the rest of the world.

Rick is a history enthusiast, so he peppers some of his choice phrasings with interesting elements of the period, all of which cause me to caution him on making sure they serve the story. I'm also the one to try to constrain all the words in the world from escaping the corral: when we hit 8,500 big bananas—and growing—I knew we already had an upsized short story (that comes with fries); I tried to avoid adding any fatty dessert.

But I did want to ensure there was a snifter of metaphoric cognac at the finish.

Bringing It Home, While Still Shaking Hands

We rounded the corner on the thing, though at more of a trot than a gallop. It didn't proceed briskly, because each of us had to mull the other's additions, considering them in light of story tone, character development and the arc of the tale, and how best to move the narrative so it was both coherent and compelling. And so it doesn't seem like it's being written by committee.

Well, we ended up pushing poor Pinky around so he ended up almost at wit's end—but we can do that: he's just a character, not a collaborator. With your collaborators, you have to be much more subtle in your manipulations. Right, Rick?

It's a fun story, with playful language but some serious events, and came in a bit over 13,000 words, so it's got some chunky chunks. I'm shopping it around now.

Perhaps you've worked with another person in writing a story—did everybody live? (Well, among the writers, that is.)

[Update: Rick must be a smooth talker. It took two years, but the long short story is now a 96,000-word novel, my third, which I'm editing now. We are still friends. Until the other day, when he mentioned that he thought it would make a good trilogy.]

How to Write After Midnight

Ha! You thought I'd open with a clever bon mot about cocaine here, didn't you? Silly! I'm going to do that *later* in my explanation. Here we'll go from collaboration with authors to collaboration with your own constitution: First we need to talk about the best time of day to write, and here I'm discussing business writing foremost, but these pastoral grounds can be walked by fiction writers for pleasure as well.

As for the best time to write, simple: Any time you can. Of course, if you're a freelancer like me, some projects require you to grind through successive hours, some can be grazed over a period of days, a paragraph here and a transitional phrase there, and some can be surveyed and then dispatched: I saw the hill of that essay, I saddled up my sentence steed, and I surmounted it, verily!

In that regard, learning how to parcel out your time when you're working on multiple projects is a valuable skill, and one that will endear you to your clients. It has taken me a while to be able to judge how long it will take me to edit a 200-page book, write a case study or come up with an ad's headlines, but now I'm much more comfortable about projecting (and meeting) deadlines. Until it's second nature, it's a good habit to track how long it takes you to work with a certain type of writing. One good method with new clients is if you're given something lengthy to write or to edit, work on the assignment for an hour or two to see what it tastes like, and you'll be better equipped to know when you'll finish eating. Don't give them your milestone schedule until you've snacked on the copy a bit.

Morning Becomes Electric (Coffeemaker)

Related to how much time you can or must spend on a project is what times are most suitable for the spending. I'm a morning guy, love to get up early, coffee in bed with a magazine to start the day, and then to the computer before 7. Unless there is something truly pressing, I'll often sift through email, glance at the news, vomit over the news, and then begin work on whatever's workable. However, as I discussed in the Distractions chapter, I no longer feverishly check my email 100 times a day, and also begin some days by immediately writing, whether it's for a story or a client.

Now when I say *working,* I mean working with clients if I have some, or working on essays or magazine/newspaper pieces if I don't—or a combination when everything's clicking. I normally have a number of queries out to various editors, and also some just at the note-taking stage. Some of the material that goes into a query is boilerplate (like your writing credentials/clips and your sign-off), so if you know well the core of your proposed article, the meat of the query can be massaged (oooohh!) a bit and then quickly stitched with the boilerplate. It might take as little as 30 minutes to write an article query, so if you find a gap in your day, why not? Of course, it might take 30 *months* for an editor to answer your query, but we won't address those sins here.

Back to those morning pages: I write with more focus in the morning, and with renewed focus after the afternoon coffee, but not with any real afternoon sustain. Thus, when my monitor's eye begins to look as bloodshot as my own, I start to crank down its shade in the waning afternoon hours. Then, I'll often do the busywork of cleaning out the inbox, boxing with the outbox, and wondering if I need Botox. I've never been one of those types that can merrily scribble away in the evening hours. I'm both fascinated and horrified by (and middlin' jealous of) those industrious souls who can bang out another five or six hours of writing after the five o'clock cocktail-hour bell has rung. (Though perhaps my religious adherence to that magic hour is what makes liquid all my after-hours writing resolve?)

In the Midnight Hour (Softly Snoring)

So, how to write after midnight? There is that cocaine that I was talking about earlier. But since that stuff makes me sneeze out automobile parts, I'd rather sleep. The only way I can write after midnight is to let the pinball machine of my brain zing around the bumpers and *ping-ping-ping* the lights while I snooze. I really have found that if you nest on a writing problem in the sunlight hours, you'll sometimes find a fresh egg of a writing solution in the morning. Of course, that doesn't help when you need a gross of eggs to finish a book, but it might help you realize that your main character should be named Zeke and not Arbogast.

(Oh yeah, I do keep a notepad by my bed and indeed I have jumped up to madly scribble an idea a'borning. But so often when I've eagerly scanned it in the morning, I see that I've inscribed something like "Blizzard muffins not naysayers. Harken Wheaties. Bilge, breathless, truth.")

Better wait for that morning coffee ...

Cacography and the Squinting Writer

But even when I drink lots of coffee, I still can't read my handwriting. To wit: I love the word *cacography*. And that affection is amplified because it has an obverse term, *calligraphy*.

I say the obverse, because the two words aren't precise opposites of one another, but rather counterparts. But your fervid brain is saying, "Why Tom, *why* do you love *cacography?*" Because the word has an almost rude sound, a yanking of the earlobe, that works well for me—I have wretched handwriting, and "cacography" serves to describe it in sound and fury.

But the real direction of this section isn't toward ear-twistings. I mentioned cacography because I wanted to talk about writing tools, and one of the most natural—though less enamored of keyboard clatterers today—is the pen. However, because my handwriting is such a cruelty to the eye, no matter if I painstakingly slow the cursive motion or speed it up, or ply it with bourbon, it always comes out as sadistic scratchings, the Caligula of cacography.

However, I do still take notes by hand when I'm mulling over an article or story, or sometimes just single words that are designed to later prompt an image or situation. Sad are the times when I've gone back to my notes and read "*Xdz?mph*" or some other transmogrification.

Does This Macbook Make Me Look Fat?

So, my writing tool in the broadest sense is my Macbook Pro, a couple of iterations of which have been my companionable computers for a number of years. The specific applications I regularly used to wrest words from the ether are Microsoft Word or TextEdit, Apple's built-in word-processor. (Ah, "word processor"—think blender experiments that render smoothies of beef tongue, lightbulbs and turn-signal lamps.) Many people decry, and with good reason, the tyranny and arbitrary nature of Word, but I have been using it for so long that it's second nature to me, unnatural nature that it is. But when I just want to write notes without the overhead of a bells-and-hellacious-whistles word-churner like Word, I use TextEdit. But head to the hills below to see what I used to write this book.

The Write Tool for Working Words

But first, speaking of Mac vs PC ...

I've done a lot of pruning of the trees, bushes and vines on our property. We've got six or seven fruit trees, many of them upwards of 50 years old, a good percentage of them showing the wear of years. I use various tools, but the one that's most reliable is the tree saw in the photo above. It's a simple device: a long serrated blade screwed to a five-foot pole. The serrated blade curves toward the sharp tip, so you can insert it at an angle into the tight crotch of a branch and if need be, cut in short, quick motions.

One interesting thing about this saw is that it's at least 50 years old too, but it whistles through the branches of the varied trees, no matter the wood's hardness or bulk. My girlfriend Alice's farmer father gave the saw to me, a bit before his death. He also gave me a much more modern tree saw, a nice lightweight aluminum one, with a telescoping height-adjusting pole. That one I gave away. The old one is so balanced, so sound and so fundamental to its purpose that it made no sense to have the fancy one.

Pruning a bit back made me think of the tools I use more often than saws: the software tools I use to prune words. I was a copyeditor in the mid-80s for a big software company, and they had developed their own word processor. It was DOS-based, of course; the earliest, miserable versions of Windows had recently come out, and there was a DOS-based Word, but the owner of my company hated Microsoft, so he had to develop his own program to spite it. But I'd never used a word processor at all, so using the clumsy keyboard-defined field codes for headlines, bolding and italics still seemed amazing to me.

Word Fattens Up, Walks Sideways Like a Crab

But six months later, the company sprang for Macintosh Plusses for the editors, and using the graphical interface, pulled into place by a mouse's tail, made words on the page work so much better for me. I worked for other software companies in the 90s, when Windows and Word became entrenched, so I moved through the various iterations of Word, both Mac and Windows, because that was the tool within the world I worked. I tried a number of word workers through time—Wordstar, WordPerfect, WriteNow, and other simpler text editors—but because I worked in corporate environments, with seemingly invariant and unmediated corporate standards, Word was the de facto player.

So habituated was I to using Word that even when I became a full-time freelancer, many years ago, I continued to use Word, though by this time, it had become a lumbering code-monster with nine heads, coming in with zillions of templates, add-ons, graphical-handling (and crashing) features and menus with endless sub-menus—kind of like the Cadillac of Johnny Cash's I wrote about earlier that was composed of the parts of twenty Caddies from twenty different years.

Having to Use a Sled to Lug Your Word Processor Around

Now, there are multiple opportunities to shed myself of Word: many other programs, like OpenOffice, can save in Word's old .doc format (though the newer .docx can be problematic). But I've become so used to Word's ways, bloated as they are, that I haven't wanted to spend the time in learning a new program, and I don't want to worry about possible conversion problems for my corporate clients. So I continue to muddle with Mac Word 2011, itself an aging tree.

But for blog posts? I always use the quick and easy TextEdit, the text editor that comes with the Mac OS. It's clean and lightweight, like that pruning saw, and does simple tasks squarely and reliably. There's no aluminum involved.

The Noble Scribe

However, this book is being written (in real time, like, *now!*) in an enhanced writing tool: Scrivener, which is a database-style application that lets you arrange, search and manipulate documents, text snippets, outlines, images and more without opening a rack of individual documents. I used it earlier when working on my newest novel.

Because I've been saving the novel chapters as individual files, I keep going back and opening them separately to remember some earlier details about a character or situation, and that's clumsy. Almost cacographous.

A tool like Scrivener lets you poke around in a bunch of associated documents and find which one has the red socks and which one the blue, without going through the drawers one by one. And it lets you color-coordinate. I originally had my Writing Voice chapter as chapter three in this book—with Scrivener, deciding to move it up to be chapter one was a three-second thing.

Shakespeare Didn't Use Scrivener—Why Should I?

Let's talk a bit more about Scrivener.

But first, let's dispatch with the subhead question first: I'm not Shakespeare. No, no, don't try to soothe my oozing writer's wounds, I can take it. Aside from that ounce of obviousness, there's this: no coders had the sense to put together Scrivener in Shakespeare's day—in fact, his choices of apps (basically a quill pen and maybe some foolscap) were pretty bare bones. He didn't do too badly with them, though.

But I think if good Will had access to the program, he would have found lots to like in its flexibility in shifting and sorting blocks of text, storing character descriptions and synopses, organizing scenes into relationships, and storing a repository of reference materials like live links and images. Willie would probably like being able to export to ebook formats too: King Lear would make a Kindle's screen crack with its stormy scenes.

I've only used the program for a novel and a long short story, and this book (and no, I'm not pimping any affiliate marketing here), so I can't go deeply into its considerable feature package. But just in playing with it a bit, let's look at it from a benefits standpoint: When you are composing long or complex documents, many are the times you want to bring up a specific section of text for comparison and verification with another—say to ensure that you had a character's age set in an early phase of an novel, and wanted to confirm that correct age in a later instance. It's a cinch to bring up disparate parts of a long document side-by-side in Scrivener.

Speaking of characters, if you're the kind of writer who builds a detailed profile of a character in a background document, the database structure of Scrivener means you can bring up a character study in a moment to review it against how you've rendered a character's behavior in a scene. You can change the character's profile, or change the scene or both. The Reference areas of the application lend themselves to the storage of URLs, images and data snippets relevant to the project. And if you were midway through a project started in another word processor or text editor, importing is easy, as is exporting back out, including some nifty formatting tools.

Why Now, Oh Scrivener?

I've written a couple of novels and a book of short stories without bothering to use a tool like Scrivener—why now? A couple of reasons: first, I'd heard great word-of-mouth report from writers who delighted in the program. But are those the ravings of people who just want to geek out with slick software, and not pointed to the ultimate outcome, the writing itself? I'll find out.

I moved to the software because the new novel I'm outlining in my soggy head will be an interconnected series of short stories, all intended to have a thematic coherency. A program like Scrivener, which lets you jump back and forth through long skeins of text, move and merge elements around in a jiffy, and organize and edit lots of contributive character and scene info is perfect for the work I envision. If only it would do the writing for me.

(One caveat though: when you do get to the Compile tool, if you have some specific formatting needs for ebooks, the depth of the tweaking can be puzzling. I took a long while—including lots of Help file puzzling and Googling—trying to get the output for this book right on the headers and line spacing and special formatting levels. I had to move it into Calibre to get the tweaks twerked.)

Tequila and Cookies: Writing Perks to Push Your Pages

Let's go from the rewards of good writing tools to writing rewards (and why you should give yourself some): As I sat hunched in my dank writing grotto, and tried to figure out a way to move my mouse so that the 40-pound chains that kept me at my desk wouldn't rattle so, I pondered the rewards of writing. No, no, not those tinhorn rewards like a Booker or a Pulitzer or a Nobel, where you are forced to podium-prattle about authorial intention while you die inside over errant exposure of your nose hairs to the functionaries seated below. No, too tedious those rewards—I turned them all down, a polite click on the phone.

The rewards in question are the spurs, the goads, the carrotiest of carrots: the *in medias res* rewards you give (or deny) yourself while you are writing, or after a writing bridge has been crossed. The system of checks and pizzas, er, balances, by which you induce yourself to squeeze out another chapped chapter or even a single soggy sentence. What are those rewards? Do they work? (And does this punctuation mark make me look fat?)

Cauterize Your Writing Wounds

Don't start with me that the writing is its own reward. Downy thoughts those, but we all know that writing is a disemboweling, by ravening wolverines wielding jagged scalpels. So let's discuss how to cauterize those wounds, but with sugar, not fire. Perhaps all it takes is a physical shift:

• Conventional rewards are labeled unhealthy, so after you've mapped out a stirring scene, you might take a yoga break. Wait, a YOGA break? Sheesh, if that's a reward, bring me some annual reports to edit, with frosting.

• What about even-steven: finish a chapter, finish a cookie. But if you're chapter-quick, that's a lot of cookies. And will the cookie lose its savor and become two cookies? That could slide to sloppy excess: Finish a good sentence—tequila shooters, all around!

• Go old school, and turn to Whitman: issue a resounding barbaric yawp to celebrate yourself. But don't frighten the cat. (Writers should have cats; if you don't have one, you can check one out from the library.)

• You could avoid all these calories and the caterwauling, and maybe take a Twitter break. But is that a real reward, anyway? (Plus, one hears that Twitter causes loss of focus and unfitness for complex sentence building.)

Not sure. Don't know. Yep.

The Tortuous Self-Negotiation

Writing can be a tortuous negotiation with yourself; it's so rare for a writer's inner critic to say, "Man, I nailed it this time. Franzen, step back!" Instead we often have the reaction I had when I recently finished a novel: *Man, I'm glad that's over.* But that's ending things not with a yawp, but a whimper, to borrow from T.S. Eliot. Besides, it's never *really* over, is it?

The old Catholic in me feels guilty about rewards. But it's not natural for me to turn to the Good Book for solace, unless perhaps it's one from Henry Miller, who could ride exuberance's horse not until it was tired, but was ecstatic. Henry probably didn't trouble himself about whether he should dole out little rewards to himself for writing; he was too busy typing away.

Maybe I have it all wrong: maybe the writing *is* its own reward.

I've always liked this quote from F. Scott Fitzgerald, "My own happiness in the past often approached such an ecstasy that I could not share it even with the person dearest to me but had to walk it away in quiet streets and lanes with only fragments of it to distill into little lines in books ... "

There it sounds as though the highest happiness is expressed in those dancing little lines. Of course, when you know the context of the quote, from Fitzgerald's extended essay on his own descent into despair in "The Crack-up," perhaps the reward example is ambiguous.

Who Trusts a Happy Writer?

I don't trust those happy writers anyway. Writing still feels like work to me, grunting when you move around a paragraph, probably because it's built like a stack of sliding bricks rather than the gossamer wings you intended. So do reward yourself when you get a good set of bricks in place.

If tequila and cookies makes you toss your cookies, make your reward a brisk walk, a cheery call to your mother, the purchase of a 39-acre estate in the Hamptons. (I so hoped to be born the scion of a dynastic family, but I comfort myself by knowing all that scionizing must be quite tiring.)

Give yourself a little something after you turn a corner in your writing, and you'll be able to hit the gas for those long writing roads that lie ahead.

Giving Your Writing the Business

Scuttlebutt had it that Barbara Cartland, the doyenne of romance writers, did much of her early writing at the piano, stark naked. However that strains credibility, everyone's heard of writers who insist they can't write without their ancient manual typewriters with the missing keys, or their favorite fountain pens (or maybe even a stylus and hot wax). Writers can be a peculiar lot, and it's not surprising that their composing methods can be all over the map.

You would think that the map for business writers would have to be a bit more restrictive, at least in terms of how they approach deadline destinations, but it ain't necessarily so. I'll peek here at some variegated methods that freelance writers use to get to the same place—the delivery of deadline material. Since I am a freelance writer (mostly for the tech industry), perforce my attentions will focus on my own methods. However, since I have kept the company of fellow miscreant scriveners in the tech-writing world, I'll toss in a couple of contrasting approaches.

One sidestep I'll take is taking on the startup mentality: though you can still hear of Silicon Valley employees working 15-hour shifts, the sleeping bag rolled at the ready under the desk, with maniacal managers patrolling cubicle fields exhorting the troops to donate their iron-poor blood to the cause of one more development deadline, that's no path to writing productivity. At least *qualitatively.*

Writing in Bursts (of Bourbon)

My distaste for those fervid accounts is personal (and relevant to this account, thank god). My general view is that even with business writing, even with pressing deadlines, the stacking of ever-tottering hours of effort just results in a diminished return: your stack will topple (and so will you). This view is prejudiced by my own writing methods: I think writing is best crafted in short bursts, somewhat like synaptic patterns, the mind sending out a sheaf of arrows that hit targets, and then reloading. I recognize that sometimes you absolutely must grind out time at the keyboard (or on your papyrus), if you know that tomorrow's brochure needs an eighth page and you've only got seven, or if you're inputting "final" edits for the 10th time on a print-ready book project at 1am, but those are times when prayer or a snappy cocktail (or both) might ease you through.

What I'm addressing is where you have writing requirements for which the scope is pretty clear: this many words on this subject gets you this check. I know writers who can just bang out a first draft by sitting down and getting up hours later. For me, taking mini-breaks is the breathing of the mind after exercise: sprint through a paragraph, get up and wander to the front window to see if anyone is undressing in the neighbor's house, sprint through another paragraph, pay the invoice for that fountain pen you regret buying, sprint through ...

These writing tips tilt favorably as well for so-called "creative" writing, corralled in quotes here because I believe that business writing can be quite creative. Often, I can only work on a fictional piece in half-hour or one-hour bursts, then need to read a magazine article or wipe grime off the stove knobs or use my hair to apply polish to my shoes.

Then, when I go back to the work, the windows open again for fresh writing air. Contrary to those tech-industry beliefs, dawdling is an integral component of productivity.

Forget the Beach—Bathe Your Brain Instead

It's a laugh to have seen so many ads in tech magazines past of people at the beach with their laptops, or writing on their decks in the blazing sun ("Stay Connected All The Time With Our Wireless You-Don't-Know-How-Asinine-You-Look-At-The-Beach-Now High-Speed Thingie), as though that was incredible freedom. Nah, freedom is when your brain does the work for you while, away from the keyboard, you peel an orange: "Ah, the hollow-but-compelling marketing phrase I was looking for just appeared in my mind—a miracle!"

So, whether you need to lean back between writing jaunts and listen to Hendrix playing *Purple Haze* at bleeding-ear volume, or choose to give the cat a good five-minute grooming (whether with a brush or your tongue), consider it all part of the writing process. Whether you decide to bill your client for that "passive concentration" time is a matter for you, your accountant and your conscience, you conscientious scribe, you.

Publishing by Self and Other Fancies

I "finished" my second novel in 2013, though the tinkering has continued. Titled *Aftershock*, it's based in San Francisco, and the 1989 earthquake plays a central part in throwing—almost literally—some disparate lives together. Nobody's particularly comfortable in the book, but that's the prerogative of the author—we get to torture our characters, so that we can be better people ourselves. Or not.

But I don't want to talk about my psychological problems. (Unless you swing by with a bottle of Pappy Van Winkle's bourbon—I have ice on ice waiting for you.) I do want to briefly talk about publishing.

Briefly, because talking about the changes in publishing is an industry in itself these days, and my adding to the din won't land me any Oprah-time.

Bleary Queries

To this point, I've sent queries about my second novel to 50+ agents. Despite the publishing heavens being torn by demons, agents remain the middle defenders for those writers hungering for the traditional publishing route, with its still-credible distribution structure, now-flagging marketing support, and tarnished-yet-dimly-shiny "Look mom, some NY bigwigs bought my book" cachet.

Depending on the agent guidelines, those queries have included a couple of full manuscripts, a lot of 10–50 page excerpts, or just a synopsis and a prayer. So far, I've received 12 rejections; some of the queries are a few months' old without response, so I'll probably follow up on the best of those.

But the winds of change have blown their clichéd gusts through publishing's doors, and floors. Self-publishing no longer has the "I wrote seven poems about grandma's feet, and had them printed with a velvet cover" taint. I self-published my first novel, had a book of short stories published by a small press after that, and should no agent show real interest in my newest work in the next few months, I'll go the self-abuse route once more. (I did always love the punch line for the you'll-go-blind masturbation joke, "Hey, can I just do it long enough so I only have to wear glasses?")

Resources: Self-pub Grub

I've been reading a good deal (i.e., too much) about the publishing industry and its earthquakes in the last two years or so. Here are a few good books that have solid info on the publishing world, self-publishing and how to market your work:

Write. Publish. Repeat.
APE: Author, Publisher, Entrepreneur
The Essential Guide to Getting Your Book Published
Create Your Writer Platform

Pub Sites with Insights

And here are some sites/pundits I read regularly that provide great resources and insights into the roiling new world of publishing.

Digital Book World
Tim Grahl
Joel Frielander at the Book Designer

And if I do self-publish, this time I'll have my book edited by some professional other than myself. Woe befalls the writer, even if they are professional editors, who edit their own work. That self-abuse could take the sight from any writer's eyes, and I *already* wear glasses, so I know better now.

Pitching Copywriting Online: Throw Strikes

Let's talk about links that lead to job leads. There's a lot of low-hanging fruit on the Net for copywriters: places like oDesk and Elance post scads of copywriting jobs, the various Craig's List sites are filled with solicitations for writers, and there are a number of revenue-sharing sites that propose to give you a cut of ad revenue in exchange for article eyeballs.

The problem with this kind of fruit is that it's rotten. When you are competing with writers willing to compose a 500-word article for five dollars (such as on Fiverr), the only competition taking place is a race to the bottom. That's a deep pit from which to crawl.

However, for the judicious writer, one who is both selective both of his or her time and of the projects pitched, there could be some sweet Net fruit ripe for the picking. For instance, I'm registered on Ebyline, which hooks up writers with set-fee projects, and takes a cut when the project is completed and paid for by the client.

There's a broad range of projects there, and many of them don't pay enough (or aren't interesting enough) for me to pitch. However, there was a pitch for writing a 1,000-word piece for the premium-scotch distiller, Glenlivet, to be published on their iPad app. The app is a nicely laid-out "lifestyle" publication of travel, dining, gadgets and more.

I bid on the $500 project—handled though an intermediary, Forbes Connect. The client liked the initial draft, but wanted a deep sidebar added and a few changes. Easy enough, particularly when the Forbes person said that they'd toss in $300 extra for my trouble, without me even asking (and I was going to ask—but not for quite that much).

Here's the finished piece,[64] which landed me $800 for 1,300 words. And Ebyline handled all of the payment process, putting the dough in my Paypal account as stated. Quite recently, I had an Ebyline-assigned gig published on Forbes, which is a feather for the cap I don't wear. Two more respectably paid Forbes assignments through Ebyline have followed.

Contented with Contently, Soaring with Skyword

I've also written articles for Contently, where you put up a colorful portfolio of your published articles, which could be useful to direct potential clients to for promo, regardless of internal pitching. Contently editors check out your stuff to hook you up with potential clients, with the same take-a-cut basis as Ebyline.

---

[64] http://thecask.us.theglenlivet.com/villa-vacations/

Clients can vet your portfolio and decide if you're suitable for the project.

The business writing I did for Contently (oddly enough, about international banking, not a field I would have pretended expertise) is at an experienced copywriter's rate, and I'm discussing more future work.

Lastly, I initially wrote a couple of short pieces for Skyword, where again, you put up a portfolio, and editors contact you for writing that seems relevant to your background. That followed up with a multi-article assignment from Google that paid well (even if the process turned a bit convoluted).

Certainly, there are a lot of garbage "opportunities" out there for writers. But if you don't waste time bidding on, or accepting low-ball gigs, you can land some projects that make sense. As mentioned, I wouldn't bother with the heavily trafficked sites, where you might be sending in your bid or resume along with 1,000 other humble seekers who are also registered at 50 content-mill sites.

Considering my experiences on sites like Ebyline, Contently and Skyword, there seem to be some businesses out there that present potential work in a straightforward fashion, don't hide that they're taking a cut (usually transparent to the writer regardless), and manage the process without significant problems.

Just don't steal the jobs I'm pitching.

What, Me Work?

Besides those content "vendors" listed above, for all of you freelancers who toil in your treetop aerie, serenaded by regal raptors, and even for those who might subject their verbs to subjective verbalizations in an old Airstream, you might wonder where your next crust of bread (or better yet, that bottle of Pappy Van Winkle's Family Reserve I seem to be fascinated with) is coming from. Fret not.

That old series of tubes dubbed the Internet will whisk job listings straight to your screen, so that you can continue to work your magic behind the home keyboard like the great and terrible Oz. You won't have to go out into society job-hunting, where you might expose those accidental dreadlocks you've been cultivating. There are all manner of job sites Netwise, but I'm talking here about listings of writing jobs delivered directly to you—and they have the bonus key lime pie of being wrapped in a writer's newsletter, full of the newsiness you writer types are keen on.

Here are a few I regularly read:

Funds for Writers – No, they aren't just going to dole out dough to you—I already asked. But the free newsletter lists lots of writing grants and retreats, writing contests and job markets. Her paid version of the newsletter has even more. And Hope Clark, the woman who runs the joint, is charming. Her column is personal and always worth the read. Delivered once a week.

Writing World – Lots of good stuff on the site itself (many helpful articles in the Business of Writing section), and sections on all writing genres—what, no haiku? Very helpful editorials in the now discontinued newsletter from Moira Allen, archived on the site.

Writer's Weekly – This is the handiwork of Angela Hoy, and it gets around: as stated, "The highest-circulated freelance writing ezine in the world." Angela sends out a weekly newsletter that has a range of contract job listings for telecommuters of every stripe. (They are mostly Craig's List jobs, so caveat emptor—unless the job is just right for you, you'll have lots of competition.)

Sites (and Sights!) Galore

Those are the only sources of writing jobs on the whole Internet. Wait, did I hear you grunt in disdain? OK, true, that isn't even a quivering bacterium's ecological cloth-grocery bag's worth (say that ten times, fast) of the job listings for freelancers on the net, but dang, who's got the time to list them all?

But if you absolutely lust to look at other lists of contract writing work (and associated writing advice and resources), here are a few other job site conglomerates I flip through now and then, some listing contract work, some submission listings, some actual (gasp, no!) jobs:

Journalism Jobs
About Freelance Writing
Copyediting
The Write Jobs
Writing Career

If you see anything there about writing songs for lovelorn squirrels, buzz me—I'm a pro.

Other Rich and Juicy Writing-Related Links

The writer's life can be an isolated one, where you, sequestered near your gnat-swarming compost heap, concentrate on your compositions, in between bouts of bitterly denouncing 14-year-olds who get publishing contracts for writing YA novels about zombie-vampire aliens who look like rutabagas (albeit sexy ones).

Wait, you mean I'm the only writer forced to scribe next to the compost bin? No matter. What I'm actually getting at is that in these cyberspheric times, writers don't have to be the lonely Kafkaesque wretches that they were in the past. They can be *connected* wretches, which is so much more sociable.

In that light, I've listed below some of the sites and personas from which I get good writer's info, or where I can pull up an electronic chair and sit a spell (to be spellbound), or where I know the site's owner always provides food for thought. Any thought leftovers I just put in that nearby compost bin.

This list is by no means exhaustive, because that would be exhausting. Nah, it's just me picking among the URL wildflower patches. Please send me any good bouquets of your own if you're of a mind to.

Blogging, Copywriting, Writing Work and General Good Writing Info

A couple of these have been mentioned before, but are worth mentioning again:

Copyblogger [rolled into Rainmaker Digital]
Make A Living Writing (Carol Tice)
Peter Bowerman's Well-Fed Writer
The WriteLife
The International Freelancer (Mridu Khullar Relph)
International Freelancer's Academy
The Renegade Writer (Linda Formichelli)
Donald Maass
Ed Gandia
Men with Pens
Boost Blog Traffic
All Indie Writers
Freelance Folder
Write to Done
TheWriteLife

Idea Sparking and Entrepreneurship

Seth Godin
Jonathan Fields
MarketingProfs
Art of Non-Conformity
Itty Biz
The Fluent Self
Chris Brogan

Publishing (Self, Industry and Otherwise) and Story Structures

Joel Canfield and Someday Box (my pal!)

Porter Anderson

The Creative Penn

Realm and Sands

The Book Designer

The Writer's Dig (Brian Klems, Writer's Digest)

There Are No Rules (Writer's Digest)

Guide to Literary Agents

Steven Pressfield

Jeff Goins

Query Shark

The Story Grid

The Rejectionist

Fiction

There are lots of great sites that discuss fiction on the Net. But I'm only listing one, because they let me contribute there (and some of the other contributors are ding-dang geniuses). So nonny, nonny, nonny.

Writer Unboxed

If I forgot you among these lissome links, it's not because I don't love you any more. It's the pain pills from the hip surgery (plus the cocktails). Remind me and I'll add you.

For $100. Plus a new compost bin.

And I would put my mother on here too, but she just won't start her damn blog. Sheesh.

Can You Take a Moment for a Review?

If you enjoyed the book, I'd be grateful if you'd review it on Amazon or Goodreads. Go to the sites and Google *Think Like a Writer,* if you please.

(Of course, reviews only need to be a few sentences or so, but do elaborate if you're of a mind too. Even if you thought the work was birdcage lining; I'm tough, I can take it.)

Acknowledgements

To my mother, who showed me that through reading, I could travel to whole new worlds.

About the Author

Tom Bentley lives in the hinterlands of Watsonville, California, surrounded by strawberry fields and the occasional Airstream. He has run The Write Word (www.tombentley.com), a writing and editing business out of his home for many years, giving him ample time to vacuum.

His business projects have varied from writing website content, the full spectrum of marketing material, user documentation for software manuals, radio ads, character dialog in video games to editing coffee-table photography books. These days he's editing many novels and nonfiction works.

He's published hundreds of freelance pieces—ranging from first-person essays to travel pieces to more journalistic subjects—in newspapers, magazines, and online. (Venues include *Forbes, Writer's Digest,* the *Los Angeles Times, Writer's Market, Wired,* the *San Francisco Chronicle, The American Scholar,* and many others; he's also won a number of nonfiction writing awards.) He has an MA in Creative Writing from San Francisco State University.

He's published fiction in a number of small journals, and was the 1999 winner of the National Steinbeck Center's short story contest. His coming of age novel, *All Roads Are Circles,*[65] was published in 2011. His short-story collection, *Flowering and Other Stories,*[66] was published by AM Ink Publishing in early 2012.

He has finished two other novels and is seeking an agent (or two). Or he's going to break down and self-pub the durn things as he indicated in the chapters above.

Sign up for his writing-related newsletter and see his lurid website confessions at www.tombentley.com.

---

[65] http://www.amazon.com/All-Roads-Are-Circles-Bentley-ebook/dp/B006L3G590/

[66] http://www.amazon.com/Flowering-Other-Stories-Tom-Bentley/dp/0984580174/

42903379R00137

Made in the USA
San Bernardino, CA
11 December 2016